Unboiling the Frog

A memoir about breaking cycles,
refinement, and enduring

Sabe Anderson

Unboiling the Frog
A Memoir About Breaking Cycles, Refinement, and Enduring

Copyright ©2023 Sabe Anderson. All rights reserved.

Published by Stories From The Hearth
storiesfromthehearth.com

The information and views set out in this book are strictly those of the author and do not replace medical advice or professional services. The information provided should not be used for diagnosing or treating a health problem or disease, and those seeking personal medical advice should consult with a licensed physician.

Although the author and publisher have made every effort to ensure that the information in this book was correct at press time, the author and publisher do not assume and hereby disclaim any liability to any party for any loss, damage, or disruption caused by errors or omissions, whether such errors or omissions result from negligence, accident, or any other cause.

The author and others quoted in this book have tried to recreate events, locales, and conversations from their memory. In order to protect the privacy of the individuals mentioned, names and identifying details have been changed.

No part of this book may be reproduced or transmitted in any form or means, electronic or mechanical, including photocopying, recording, or by any information storage and retrieval systems, without written permission from the publisher.

Interior design: Elizabeth Thomas
Cover design: Sabe Anderson
Cover photo: Jen Anderson Photography

Print ISBN: 978-0-9996402-2-7
Ebook ISBN: 978-0-9996402-3-4

Printed in the United States of America

This book is dedicated to the amazing women and family in my life and to all those out there who have similar stories. There are many.

I encourage every one of you to write your story. It's a healing process and will provide value to your family, friends, and support groups.

Introduction

My name is Jared Casey, and I'm a father of five, a married man of twenty years, a Christian, and a licensed marriage and family therapist. In 2017, I co-created a company called I Am Recovery to help people struggling with addiction and mental health struggles. I'm passionate about helping people get better and stay better through meaningful living.

I met Sabe during the COVID pandemic, and I instantly admired him. We were working together to provide stable jobs to people in early recovery, and Sabe was so excited to be helping people get jobs and second chances. He would go to bat for people and mentor them like they were his own kids. One man in particular struggled with bipolar disorder and became a casualty of his sickness far too soon. Sabe wept for him, as did I.

Despite knowing Sabe as well as I did, I never realized how dark things were for him until I read this book. Sabe's struggle with bipolar disorder and addiction, once only discussed openly in abnormal psychology classrooms and behind "cold" psychologist doors, comes to life in its pages. His narrative offers a map of meaning without reservation or judgment, and his family shares their stories alongside his, offering deep insights into the struggles they have faced while living with people who suffer with mental health, addictions, and all the instability that comes from those shared burdens.

Sabe's family's story is unfortunately becoming all too common in the United States and worldwide, yet rarely is it shared with such raw multi-generational clarity. As I read, I couldn't help but think of my own family's struggles and wonder "what if?" What if Sabe's mom had had more support in the home? What if Sabe's family had given up on him? What if Sabe's father had had better recovery options? What if Sabe's spiritual leaders had been more consistently like Jesus instead of Judas?

This is a story of resilience, courage, hope, faith, and a desire to break generational patterns for his children. Sabe's autobiography shows us that we cannot keep relying on the tools of the past to solve the problems of today; however, we can build from the experiences of the past to improve today and make tomorrow more meaningful for our children.

I've worked with many people over the years who have severe mental health and addiction struggles. Many of them, like Sabe, have found their way to more meaningful and joyful lives. Many others have passed on too early or continue to suffer greatly. The differences between those who succeed and those who continue to get more hard education cannot be easily quantified. I do believe that there are forces alive and unseen all around us seeking to persuade us to do more and live better and there are forces that seek for our misery.

It's tricky, but you have to be the right kind of selfish to succeed. You have to want it all so that you can give it all away. You have to want to live, truly live—not just exist in a meat sack. You have to wake up and do God's will more than your own! Do something, anything for goodness sake, today, in this moment. It doesn't have to be a lot; just a spark will do. The bonfire is set up and ready to burn inside you. In whatever form of light and love you see God, be ready!

God will transform you into something far greater than you can make yourself. God will convert you into a messenger of hope, joy and love. God will share the weight of the pain and leave you with strength and experience so that you may help others like no others can. God will continue to provide angels seen and unseen all around you. Start seeing those angels and get to a support meeting, church, therapy, coaching, or all of the above. As they say in AA, "It works if you work it!"

It's a little shocking to have met Sabe as he is today and try to connect him to the man he describes himself to be in this book. In truth, I like him even more now that I know he is a sinner like me just trying to do the best that he can. Sabe woke up to the unfair life he was experiencing and realized it was actually incredibly unfair in his favor. He made subtle but important shifts into gratitude and awareness that have put him on a better course to reconcile with his Maker.

And his life continues on. Perhaps his bipolar symptoms will become too great, or perhaps they won't. But today, in this space in time, he's doing his best to give back and improve the future for all of us.

Jared Casey, LMFT

Preface

Life is not linear; it folds back on itself. We live with our past, and as we repeat each day, we should take the trials from that past and progress in wisdom, principle upon principle and concept upon concept. For many years, I was a conflicted soul of depression, mania, and delusions wrapped up in the shame of trying to be a follower of the gospel of Jesus Christ and a good father. I wrote this book as part of my healing and reaching out process, reviewing my past through the lens of the present.

Alcoholism is a theme that rears its ugly head in many of these stories. It became another member of our family. It tore my father from us and weighed on our souls, always there, waiting to cause pain and destruction. My dad has often said that "a bad example can be a good one." I find that sad.

But Dad's disease is one of the biggest reasons I was able to finally take control of my own illness, bipolar disorder. I hated alcohol, and when I chose to self-medicate, my choices were harder to get and much more expensive. Both factors gave me moments of sobriety and clarity, which allowed me to see my disease between the highs and lows. When you are in the grips of alcoholism, it's cheap, legal, and all-around hard to ever get a rest from.

Another big reason I was able to take control is the influence of the powerful women in my life. Perseverance is the skill and quality of someone who can love unconditionally, and you will see it time and again in this book.

I particularly want to highlight the goodness of my mother. She made all five of her sons do Cub and Boy Scouts and stay active in sports, church, and school, all while dealing with Dad's struggles and trying to build a career of her own to support her growing family. She forged ahead and defied many of the odds stacked up against her, and in doing so, her journey empowered my own.

Almost a year after Mom's passing, my brother found what seemed to be the beginning of her autobiography. I have included her words here alongside mine.

My wife, Lisa, is another person who I could never do without. She has been with me through a lot of this journey, and you can read some of her thoughts in the footnotes.

A Family Is Born

> Where to start except at the beginning?[1] Chris and I met when he was sixteen and I was fifteen. It was love at first sight for me, but I certainly did not want him to know that! Besides, I did already have a boyfriend, and in the small community that I lived in, a new boy in town was a threat. Chris was good looking, and all the girls loved him. This made him the enemy of all the boys, and the boys did everything they could to undermine him. They saw that he was eliminated from any opportunity on the sports teams, and they did everything in their power to prevent him from being accepted.
>
> Chris may have drunk ... prior to his move to Wayne County, but I am sure he drank when he moved there in order to try to fit in. He never drank around me, and I believed that he was a very religious young man (our religion forbids alcohol, tobacco, and hot drinks, including tea and coffee). I admired the diverse qualities he possessed. He was very talented musically and artistically, and he was very different from any boy I had known. I loved him for his uniqueness.
>
> We met in Richfield, Utah, in a stockyard barn as I was getting ready to show my 4-H steer. I was grooming my animal prior to taking him into the show ring. Chris claims it was love

---

[1]. This is how my mother opened her autobiography. This book combines our stories, so to signal which of us is talking, her or me, I've placed Mom's words in this boxed format.

at first sight for him as well. He always scared me a little, though; he was a little too forward with his expressions of love and I was not ready for such a big commitment. I began to engage in sarcastic and negative responses in order to prevent him from getting too close to me emotionally.

… I tried to just be friends with him and date him and others, but that did not work well and resulted in several fights between Chris and the boys who gathered together to gang against him. I witnessed one such fight in the lane close to my home while I was with him. His sister Jill was with us. These instances I have tried to suppress and forget through the years, but occasionally they surface and I feel the pain he must have felt as a newcomer at age sixteen.

… This relationship did evolve into marriage at the respective ages of seventeen and eighteen in a rushed marriage due to pregnancy. We were married a day after he graduated from high school and at the end of my junior year on May 24, 1969.

We did not spend that much time together right after we were married because I went off to summer school at the University of Utah. I had a scholarship between my junior and senior years. Chris and I would see each other about every third weekend during this time.

I lived with my sister and her husband, and I went to school during the day. Later that summer, they moved to Okinawa and I was left to find an apartment for myself, which I did with the help of Mother and Dad. After a week or so, I found a family that was in need of a nanny. They provided board and room and a small stipend ($15 a week), which relieved me of the expenses of a rental and gave me a little spending money. This allowed me to be available during the day to babysit and clean the house and then attend night school at South High in Salt Lake City, Utah. With the combined high school and college credits, I was able to graduate from high school at Thanksgiving time in what should have been my senior year.

… On December 15, 1969, Dalton Tyler was born. Dalton

> was a beautiful and healthy baby. He was the light of my life. Our lives together as a little family held a lot of promise for me even though we were young and had a lot of foundation to build in terms of education and careers.

So begins my mom's autobiography and her adult life. Decades later, in her last few months sitting in my living room, Mom cried as she told me how these early events propelled her to learn more about her Maker, forgiveness, and overcoming the odds.

She and Dad began attending Snow College, then transferred to Utah State University a year later. They shared one class there, chemistry. I'm told that during one particular chemistry exam, Dad passed Mom's desk, grabbed her test, and put his unfinished questions down on her desk in its place.

Many in Mom's small community wondered why she wanted to attend college at such a fragile time in her life. "Just stay home and be a God-fearing and obedient housewife," they would say. But my mother wanted a better destiny for her family. It was the mantra of her life.

> Pursuing college was always an uphill battle. Chris and his parents were against college, as he and they wanted him to stay on the farm and build a family business. My family, on the other hand, was encouraging and supportive of education. This created tension between the families and us.
>
> Each summer, we would move home to the farm and spend three months farming and helping Chris's father. Each fall, the battle would begin on whether we would stay on the farm or go back to school.
>
> … Chris's dad would pay him about $300 a month, which was barely enough to sustain us through the summer and certainly not enough to save to pay for any college expenses. After the third summer, I went to pay the rent for the quarter, which was $75 a month, and I returned home with only pennies remaining. At that time, I told Chris that he was free to go home in the future but I would never return to work on the farm.

Chris's dad always wanted him to be in the business with him, but he was unwilling to ever create a business plan or partnership documents. He did not handle his business in a business-like way, and therefore I was unwilling to pursue a business relationship. This attitude, of course, has created ill will within the family and has been a source of contention through the years.

During our time [at Utah State University] in Logan, Chris never cared about school and was always flunking a course or two each semester, it seemed. This caused great angst in me, as I was sure he needed an education in order to adequately support a family. These were difficult years for me in trying to balance raising Dalton and going to school and getting good grades. I was very appreciative of the opportunity, and Chris loathed it. We argued frequently over this issue.

We supported ourselves with college grants and loans, which I always applied for and managed.

Chris played in a country western band. I believe this was a wrong choice, as it placed Chris directly in the line of fire of alcohol and people who consumed it. However, he made $50-$75 a night, which was good money then. This money, he kept, managed, and used to fund his activities, [rarely contributing] to the household income. A pattern I identified early on with my own behavior is that I never wanted to be a financial burden on Chris, and so I was always finding ways to contribute to the income and support the family and myself (enabling).

I remember this time of our life as being very argumentative, again with alcohol at the center. He would spend time with the guys and gambling at bars [and doing] who knows what. I hated the lifestyle, and I hated him for what he was doing to himself and our marriage.

Chris also worked at a gas station during these years, and this was his employment at the time our second son, Sabe, was born.

Five years after Dalton was born, on June 30, 1974, I was born in Logan, Utah. The hospital, which caught fire and burned down years later, recorded and listed my sex as female on my birth certificate, something I didn't find out until I was eighteen years old. At the time, males were automatically registered to serve the United States in case of a war. Since I was "female," I was not.

> Chris played in the band for approximately four to five years [before that] career abruptly ended one night. His father and mother were visiting from out of town and he did not return home as usual around 2:00 a.m. I went looking for him (which was not unusual) and found him outside the bar in a truck with another woman. This created a very awkward situation, and he never went back to the bar and played again. He offered excuses to me and again denied any wrongdoing. I, of course, believed him. I wanted all to be well with my life, my marriage, and my family, so I did not pursue it any further.
>
> We spent almost seven years in Logan, Utah, going to school and working. I taught school there after graduation for about two years. Chris eventually dropped out of college and pursued leasing a farm in Mendon, Utah, called the Spring Creek Ranch. This venture was short-lived, less than a year. When we returned from Christmas break, the oil had run out of the furnace, the pipes had busted, and water flooded the apartment we were living in. This apartment was at the top of a barn and it was the dead of winter, so we moved back into town. We actually stayed with some friends for a few days while we located an apartment. This was a difficult and embarrassing time.
>
> At this time, I was in graduate school. Chris began looking for work and came up with the idea of starting a western tack store in Richfield, Utah. This was closer to home and our families, and I was against the idea. However, he was insistent and pursued it. At this time, I was pregnant with our third son (Ethan Travis). I abandoned graduate school and followed him to Richfield, where he followed his dream of the tack store.

Dad eventually opened a saddlery shop selling custom leather goods, saddles, boots, and other western gear. He has always had an entrepreneurial spirit and desire to work for himself, while Mom was more traditional. She taught school and so had a stable income and provided our family with health insurance. On the side, they both became independent agents of the same multi-level marketing company, Shaklee, selling health and beauty products.

One more brother, Joshua, was born during this time. Ethan was only two years younger than me, and Josh was two years behind Ethan.

> We purchased our first home for $38,000, a large sum for me. I did not know how we would make the $350 house payment every month.
>
> I cannot remember exactly how long the store lasted, probably not more than two years. Chris had two partners in the store, and the partnership did not work out and he was unable to sustain everything on his own. He eventually pursued other endeavors, including a gasohol still invention that his father was a partner in and a sheep dip that was eventually banned by the EPA. Each of these opportunities had large potential according to him, and [they all failed] for one reason or another (always because of the faltering or failings of others beside himself, according to him). During these years, I found ways to contribute to our support through Shaklee and also teaching school at South Sevier High School.

Our home in Richfield was a one-story brick house with a cinder block fence. We had a small yard in front, big enough for four boys to play in, and we lived across the street from a large park, baseball field, and community swimming pool. It seemed like a safe haven for us, and there were a lot of neighborhood kids who were our ages. I have fond memories of biking on the streets, swimming, going to the park to play basketball and baseball, and playing football with Dallas Cowboys helmets and footballs that we received from Santa. There was also an infamous Daisy BB gun that we would shoot at squirrels, birds, glass bottles, and each other. Later on when we lived in Virginia, I used that BB gun to shoot my brothers with balled-up tin foil. They hated it.

Poor Ethan had several accidents as we played and roughhoused. One day, two-year-old Ethan was following me out the door of the house while a family friend who had just visited was in her truck, about to pull out of our narrow driveway. Unaware of this, I hurried out and yelled and waved to Ethan, who was wearing a football helmet, to come across the driveway. What happened next was terrifying. As Ethan crossed the driveway, he was struck by the vehicle. It completely rolled over him, cracking his football helmet, slicing a huge gash into his back, and leaving his body motionless and limp on the other side. He was quickly rushed to the hospital, where he received stitches down his back. It was a true miracle that he was wearing the helmet.

On another occasion, the four of us were playing baseball on our front lawn. Dalton was behind the plate, waiting for a pitch, and when it came, he swung the bat as hard as he could. The ball headed straight toward Ethan in the outfield, flew just over the tip of his glove, and hit him square in one eye. You could hear the crack from across the field, and Ethan dropped to the ground in tears. His eye was swollen shut for weeks afterward as he nursed a fracture.

Josh also had his challenges. As an infant and toddler, he would hold his breath when he cried. One time, he was standing on a chair in the middle of the kitchen and crying, either because he was hungry or because he wanted Mom's attention. He began to hold his breath and eventually passed out and fell off the chair, crashing to the floor.

But the biggest scare was when Josh was put to bed one night struggling to breathe. Mom checked in on him later in the night, and he had turned blue. She called the doctors at the local hospital. They were unable to diagnose or treat him, and it was evident that he needed to be taken to Salt Lake City in an ambulance that was equipped to handle SIDs. Josh was lucky to make it.

> In both of these incidences [Ethan being run over and Joshua's breathing trouble], Chris was a pillar of strength and helped me through. ... He stood by my side with Ethan and he also nurtured Joshua back to health day after day in the hospital while I sat numbly by. Joshua was born cesarean, and I was weak and exhausted. Chris is a sensitive and caring father, and

> he demonstrated his love physically and emotionally. This has always endeared him to me.

But there was also a lot of yelling and contention when Dad would come home at night. He spent late nights out with the guys, playing cards and drinking alcohol. I believe Mother tried shielding us from their disagreements. There seemed to be a double standard with Dad's group of friends: Many of the men would attend the Church of Jesus Christ of Latter-day Saints on Sundays and then go against the church's standards during the week. And it wasn't only my father and his friends—my mother's father and brothers, who lived nearby, also struggled with addiction and this double-standard lifestyle.

My mom's father was diagnosed with bipolar disorder when he was fifty, around the same time he and my grandma divorced. He was an outstanding businessman and well loved, a man who had helped many farmers with irrigation design and getting water to their farms. He taught my mom and her siblings how to work hard and to have respect for cattle ranching and the environment. He always wanted his kids to have what they wanted by working hard and achieving their goals. But after he was diagnosed, he ruined his reputation through many drunk, bipolar incidents. I heard stories about him doing things like driving a truck in his underwear and hat in a delusional state or wandering the airport trying to figure out how to get an airplane to fly to Hollywood so he could guest appear as a model on the *Tonight Show*. In his depressive states, he would lie on the couch for weeks without moving.

As I grew up, there were only a handful of times when I spent a considerable amount of time with my grandpa. We went fishing once, and he showed us how to gut a fish. I remember having breakfast with him at the town diner on Main Street. He smoked and smelled of beer, and I remember thinking of him as our cowboy grandpa.

He sought help from doctors to deal with his depression/bipolar disorder before the term "bipolar disorder" was even used. Back then, it was termed "manic depression." He had phases of positive mental health when he stayed on his lithium, but after a while, he would decide he felt better and stop taking his meds and his life would turn for the worse.

My uncle Michael, my mother's brother, was probably bipolar too, but he was not diagnosed. He was companions with Mitt Romney during his church mission in France and was a dynamic individual, but bipolar disorder and alcohol got the best of him until he died of cancer.

I loved all my uncles and my mother's father, and they were all great men in many ways. They were my role models, and we had many fun times with them. That was part of the problem, because my mother really struggled with their behavior. Her marriage was not good, and I believe she simply wanted a new life.

2,000 Miles Ahead

I remember one night I went looking for Chris and found him with Caleb Jones and Arden Lynfesty dragging Main. I chased them down and went and pulled Chris out of the truck by the hair of his head. This is when I realized I was behaving crazy and needed to do something drastic to break this sick cycle.

At this point in time, I did not realize that alcoholism was the problem. I thought just the opposite: that we had so many problems (mainly financial) that if only they would go away, the alcohol would stop.

During these years, Chris bought a brand-new Ford truck that was eventually repossessed and he lost his business and refused to get full-time work. He bounced checks and would borrow money from people as part of business ventures. He did this with his Uncle Ira, Tim Crawford, and countless others. I recorded [the debts] in a journal and carried it around with me for years, trying to figure out how I would ever make restitution for all his business endeavors. I do not think he has ever paid one of these individuals off, and they were too big for me to tackle, especially since I had major responsibilities with the boys.

Chris did not take much responsibility for the boys or going to church, and he eventually even avoided family functions. I tried to leave a couple of times, but I really had nowhere to go and I refused to go home to my parents. Even if I did go

> somewhere in Utah, it would not have been far enough away from him.
>
> At this time, my parents divorced. My family was in a lot of pain, and I did not like how things in my marriage were turning out. I had four sons, and I determined if they were raised with the role models that surrounded them and turned out like any of them, I would consider my life a failure.
>
> I was determined to take them far away from these circumstances. I thought a geographic cure would work. I had one friend who lived outside of Utah, an Iranian friend, Esther, who I'd met at Utah State University. Esther lived in Washington, D.C. I had visited her a couple of times, and I liked the Washington, D.C., area. Chris visited there with me once and I tried to talk him into considering moving there and starting our lives over again. He placated me by saying he would look into it, but he never took it any further.
>
> In the fall of 1981, I decided I had had enough of the lifestyle in southern Utah and I made plans to move east to Washington, D.C. I had a garage sale and made plans to leave during the Christmas break in order to get there in time for the kids to start school in the new year.

And so, during the school winter break in 1981, my mom's father showed up with a U-Haul. Mom told us to pack our bags and help move what we could into the truck because we were moving to the East Coast.

Her plan was quite simple: She would drive her car with three of the boys and her father would drive the U-Haul with the other one of us until we landed in Virginia. Mom had $2,000 in her bank account and a lot of faith that everything would work out.

Dalton was devastated. He excelled in football, basketball, and baseball, was on all-star teams, and had many friendships he was leaving behind.

Ethan didn't want to leave his bike. He kept taking it up the ramp of the U-Haul before it was time, and someone kept having to take it out again to make room for the more oversized items.

Josh was still too little to know what was really happening, and as for me, I was very upset when I found out that my father wasn't coming with us. I remember hiding in a closet, crying, not wanting to go, and my mom finding me to pull me out.

This was the beginning of a "survival mode" for me, an emotional disconnect that lasted from ages seven to eighteen. I have blocked a lot of things out. I wanted my dad to be normal, and I felt bitter toward my mom for not being more of the homemaker that our church kept trying to teach us a woman should be. She was the discipliner, she worked too much, and she was stressed out a lot.

Mom wanted everything packed before Dad came home that day. I don't remember what happened when he did, but I do remember that after we hit the road, I spent my time looking out the back window at every mile that passed, thinking of him.

> Three days after Christmas, on December 28, Chris left the house to go to work. I cannot even remember what he was calling work at that point. Anyway, I went and got the biggest U-Haul truck I could rent, backed it into my driveway, and proceeded to pack up the house. My dad came to help me, and he agreed to drive the truck across the country, as I would be driving the car. We worked all day to get the house packed up and loaded into the truck. There was room for everything. I left Chris's clothes and some food, as Dalton was crying, wondering what his dad was going to eat. A neighbor came over and wondered what they could do. I asked them to take the Christmas turkey and make sandwiches for the journey.
>
> At 5:00 p.m., Chris returned home (he had been drinking) to find an empty house. He began to create a scene with my father, accusing him of being a poor example [because he tried] to assist me. I called his attorney, my cousin Zack Harrison, and asked him to come and get Chris so there would not be a scene.
>
> About this time, Chris's mother and brother showed up for a social visit and were visibly upset by the situation. I tried to explain to them that I could no longer take the lifestyle we were living and I wanted to get out. It was a very emotional time, with Sheryl saying I could not take the grandchildren she had helped to raise. Zack came and talked with Chris and I left with

> the four sons.
>
> I was traveling over the mountain to stay with Mother the first night, and Sabe, who at the time was seven years old, said, "I know why we are leaving. It is because Daddy drinks, right?"
>
> At that moment, I knew he had a drinking problem, but I never equated it to alcoholism.
>
> We trekked across the country for the next four days, which was quite a venture. I crossed the country with all the household goods in tow, in the dead of winter, and managing the four boys. We traveled by day, retired early at night, and I would put the boys in their pajamas and find the nearest laundromat to launder their clothes. I will not write the details of that journey here, but I can say that even though I had only $2,000 in my pocket, no place to live, and no job, I had faith that everything would work out for our good.
>
> We arrived in the Washington, D.C., area on New Year's Day, 1982. Karim, Esther's husband, helped us find a place to live and actually co-signed on the lease with me for the townhouse on Generation Drive. We moved in during a snowstorm, and several members of the church showed up to assist us.

To say Reston, Virginia, was a shock to us small-town cowboys is an understatement. The homes looked modern, and they were all connected. The thing I hated most about that was that we could hear our next-door neighbors through the walls. That circumstance hadn't existed in Richfield.

Reston is a planned community with walking/bike paths, community swimming pools, lakes, and a few golf courses. To us, it was a large city. Our new home didn't have a yard with grass, so we had to go to a field across the street to play. There were trees everywhere with patches of woods to hide in and play, but Virginia didn't have tall mountains, and outdoor activities were fewer than in Utah. There weren't farms, horses, or areas where we could shoot guns in a safe place. When we did shoot guns, it was deep in the woods or out of a back window of our home where no one could see.

As I walked up to the school for the first time, I felt like I was on another planet. It was built into a hill and had large solar panels above the entrance that made it look like a spaceship. I became scared of my teacher due to her stern, cranky ways.

Between the foreign environment and having a scary teacher, no dad, and no friends, I wasn't feeling the greatest. Added to that was that as a baby and in my early childhood years, I had sucked my thumb. As a consequence, I had buck teeth and earned the nickname "Sabertooth." I remember being very self-conscious about my teeth after we moved, and I would lean on them with my thumb, pressing them back over time. That did the trick, and I saved my vanity and thousands of dollars in braces.

Mom's first source of income when we arrived was babysitting local kids. Many families had dual incomes, and "tending" was badly needed. Dalton was often asked to watch us boys so she could watch other kids. One day, we headed out to the pool and someone called social services and complained that we were not with an adult. Later that week, Mom was visited by a social worker assigned to my family. I remember it being very embarrassing to my mother, who was trying to survive the best she could. To be called out by a neighbor must have enraged her.

Sports kept us busy after school and was a good outlet for young boys' aggression and frustrations. Each fall, Mom signed us up for football. Winter was basketball.

Still, I was disconnected and angry about life and often found myself getting in trouble and doing mean things to neighborhood kids. One afternoon, some of us were hanging out at the bottom of the development and one of the kids was riding his bike toward us. We had a long stick from one of the nearby trees, and as he rode his bike closer, I grabbed the stick and threw it into the spokes of his front wheel. He flew over the handlebars and hit the ground. We laughed.

On another occasion, we found a gallon of gasoline and decided to set a fire in the woods. We gathered sticks and leaves from the surrounding dead foliage, and after we gathered what we thought was enough, we poured gasoline on the wood to enhance the explosion. When we lit it, there was a massive ball of flame that engulfed more than that pile of wood and quickly grew out of control. We ran out of the woods, screaming for help. Others saw what was happening and called the fire department. Fortunately, no people or homes were harmed. I didn't seem to learn my lesson, though, because I set fires two other times in different neighborhoods that we lived in.

Six months after we arrived in Virginia, Dad borrowed enough money to follow us.

> Within days [of our initial move], Chris had flown across the country and contacted our mutual friend in order to find us. I was furious with him; I had not come all that way across the country by myself with four sons to have him get on an airplane and fly out! I refused to see him, and I do not know how many days he stayed, but I talked Esther into insisting that he go home. He did, but then he returned again shortly thereafter. This time, Esther talked me into letting him at least see how the boys were doing. I agreed to meet him, and the rest is history. He stayed with us and we tried to pick up our lives.

The First Intervention

Dad continued to struggle with his addiction to alcohol, but he made efforts to get a job and help provide for our struggling family. His first job was as a shoe salesman in Georgetown, and I remember him bringing home fancy shoes at different times.

When I was eight years old, I was baptized by someone other than my father, which is abnormal (but not unheard of) in our church. Dad wasn't living the commandments well enough to do it, so some strange man baptized me instead.

I often felt embarrassed by how Dad would act in front of my family and friends. For instance, I had a friend over one night and we were watching a movie. Dad—clearly drinking—came in, sat down, and then sarcastically raised his voice and asked my friend if he was going to eat all the popcorn. My friend quickly gave him a bowl of popcorn. There were also many times when my parents would argue. As a way to cope with both situations, I became more and more disconnected from what was happening at home.

> About three months after Chris arrived, I noticed empty liquor bottles hidden under the couch and in dresser drawers. I realized that once again I had a noose around my neck and I had nowhere to go. I had to face the problem.
>
> At this point, I found a Fairfax County social program that provided information about alcohol. I attended it and was introduced to Al-Anon. I do not remember all the details,

but I found a meeting at Christ's Church in Alexandria, close to my work, and I began to attend meetings during my lunch hour. These meetings were very helpful in providing me with the principles of the Al-Anon program, which helped me look at my options. But it took me a lot of time to take baby steps toward those options.

From 1982 to 1984, I gathered information. It was a comfort and a horror to learn that alcoholism is a disease. It was a relief to learn that I could not control it or cure it and that I did not cause it. I did learn, however, that I can contribute to it. I spent endless hours trying to figure out the difference between detachment and denial. I was never good at letting go and letting God or controlling my reactions, especially anger. I lived with constant anxiety with a compulsion to do something!

During this time, I visited a psychiatrist, talked with the bishop of my church, and gathered bottles, labeled them with the dates, and stored them in a corner in the basement to one day show the accumulated evidence of this devastating disease. I tried to learn to detach (which eludes me). One day while ironing my sons' shirts for church, I looked in the corner and my evidence was gone. Furious, I ran to Chris and asked him what he had done with the evidence. He cleverly stated he had no idea what I was talking about! To this day, that is another incident that he denies.

Incidences of his drinking continued to accumulate. One very memorable one happened one morning when I got up and was getting ready for church. I went into the dining room, and in the corner of the room on the floor was a pile of bowel movement. I do not remember my reaction, but most likely true to form, I would have yelled and screamed in anger, demoralized him, and then gone off to church with the boys in furious indignation. I probably sat through church in disbelief, not knowing what to do and hiding the situation from the world and myself. How can you even acknowledge these situations, let alone figure out what to do about them? I had tried fighting them. I had taken a geographic cure. There seemed to be no answer! I tried everything, and yet nothing changed. Nothing was better.

He would often murmur under his breath, "That's right, go learn to be like Jesus. You need it." I knew he was right; my behavior was not very Christian. But deep inside, I felt justified in these outrageous situations.

Through the help of Al-Anon, I could see that my behavior and reactions were also insane, and I did not like myself and how I was handling things. I knew I needed help. ...

During these years, Chris moved from one job to another and eventually quit working altogether. ... I had taken a job with Presidential Classroom for Young Americans, and I had to travel to Alexandria every day, which was quite a commute. However, I was grateful for the job and the steady annual income of $22,000 that somehow stretched to cover the family's needs.

By now, I was reaching out for help through Al-Anon and the church and investigating treatment. One of the things I learned was that I would need to purchase a home in my name only so we could keep Chris from coming home until he got treatment. This was a process because this was in the mid-'80s when interest rates were out of sight, around 15-18%. We had successfully sold our home in Richfield and I had about $20,000 to put toward another home, but there were several criteria: 1) I needed a home with an assumable mortgage in order to get a low rate, 2) the home needed to be large enough for four children, and 3) it needed to be within walking distance of the elementary, intermediate, and high school because I was a working mom. There was one home in Reston that qualified, and so I put a contract on it and was able to borrow another $20,000 from Mom in order to purchase it.

The day I planned to move, we had an intervention with the bishop and a representative from Meadows Recovery, which was a new center that had just opened for business. Dalton, who was fourteen at the time, and Sabe, who was nine, participated in the intervention. I took Ethan and Josh to a sitter.

Dad was told there was an important family meeting, and he must have entered the location where we were staging the intervention wondering why his two oldest kids and a strange person (the interventionist) were there to meet with the bishop, him, and Mom.

I don't remember how I felt, but I can still see the small, carpeted room. Old cloth couches lined the wood-paneled walls, and it felt dingy–unclean and uncaring. We all found a place to sit on a couch, and as we closed our eyes and bowed our heads for a family prayer, I heard a loud bang on the wall behind me. I looked up to see if anyone else had heard the noise, but no one looked up. I heard the same loud bang again at the end of the prayer, but on the other side of the room. I looked up again to see if anyone had heard, but they hadn't. Strangely, it comforted me to know something else was in that room with us. To me, it meant that everything was going to be okay.

> We were not successful in getting Chris to agree to go to treatment at that time. He refused, but I did hold true to the consequences and did not allow him to move with us that day. I do not know where he went for several days, but he would call periodically and tell me that he needed help. I would agree with him and tell him that I could not help him, but I did know where he could go for help.
>
> After several days … , he finally agreed to go for help and so I took him to the Meadows Recovery Center in, I believe, Jessup, Maryland. I had made arrangements with my insurance and the treatment was going to cost about $5,600, which was a lot of money at that time and something I could never have come up with on my own. One of my enabling patterns has always been to financially take responsibility for the family, often covering Chris's financial problems. I would say to myself, "If I just make us whole, we can start again." This has been an endless pit.
>
> As we were driving there, Chris began to negotiate with me and tell me that he was already in a program. When I asked what he meant, he asked if I remembered one night when he did not come home. He went on to say he was stopped by a cop and he refused a breathalyzer test, so they booked him in the local

jail and, as a consequence, they ordered him to participate in the Alcohol Safety Action Program (ASAP). As he talked faster, I drove, because this was just more evidence of the magnitude of the problem.

He did check into treatment, and I was relieved for twenty-eight days. I was hopeful that this would be the beginning of a different kind of life for us. I do not remember the exact time this happened, but I believe it was June 1984. Chris would have been thirty-three years old.

The family visited him every weekend, and we learned about alcoholism and its effects on the family. The boys were relatively young: Dalton fourteen, Sabe nine, Ethan seven, and Josh five. I tried to share with each what I thought was appropriate, although it was difficult and my tendency was to minimize, deny, rise above, and move on. I wanted to put distance between us and this terrible plague.

I would work all week, go to see Chris on Saturday, take the boys to church on Sunday, and begin the week all over again. This was a hectic pace, but during the week, I did find some solace and peace in knowing he was in a safe place and hopefully finding a way to have a better life.

I remember going to the rehab center and walking past my father, who was curled up on a cot next to a single window at the end of the room, vigorously shaking and sweating from going through detox. At that moment in time, I saw the reality of alcoholism. It was as if something was ravishing my father from the inside. I remember feeling his pain as I looked on.

When it came time for Chris to leave the treatment center at the end of twenty-eight days, I did not want him to come home. I wanted him to go to a halfway house. I was afraid that if he started drinking again, I would be in the same boat and I would not have any way to get him out of the house. The folks at the treatment center, however, convinced me that he had gone

> through this program and I should at least give him a chance. They assured me that they were there and supportive and would be there for a safety net. I reluctantly let him come home.

1981 to 1986 was more or less a dark time for me. I struggled in school, adjusted to the suburbs, dealt with the many disappointments of having an alcoholic father who bounced from job to job, and tried to avoid listening to my parents argue. I remember getting home from school, getting ready for football by myself, then walking back to the school for practice. I remember missing having a mother there when I came home after school. I also resented Al-Anon because it would take my mother away for one or two nights a week, and if we ever attended a meeting with her, I would see her cry. It deeply saddened me, and seeing it was too much reality for me. Now, I know that having four boys, a job, and a struggling husband must have been paralyzing and debilitating for her at times.

The only thing that seemed to be going right in my life then was sports. Dalton was an all-star in football, baseball, basketball, and wrestling, and my younger brothers and I looked up to him and wanted to do the same. I found friends through sports and enjoyed the smell of grass on the field and the feeling of winning. I learned teamwork, leadership, and how to deal with pain. As an added bonus, football practice was an outlet to hit and tackle without consequences. My internal issues had an accepted way of manifesting themselves.

What a Strange Family We Were

When Chris returned home, he did not embrace AA and incorporate it into his life. Of course, this caused great consternation with me. I think it was probably six months or so before I began to see evidence of drinking again. So of course, I contacted the treatment center right away. They informed me that because he had started drinking and failed to migrate to AA, he had broken his contract with them and there was nothing they could do.

This … infuriated me. Here I was again with him drinking, in the house with no way of removing him. And he certainly was not going to go anywhere. Well, I was not going to stand for this, so I went to a magistrate and asked for a restraining order. They asked me if he was violent. I said, "Not really, but he could be if provoked. He squeezed my arm once." (In reality, I was the violent one. Once, I took a baseball bat to him. It nearly cracked his arm.) I do not remember exactly why the magistrate did issue the restraining order, but he did. It was delivered and Chris ignored it, which meant that I had to elevate the issue to the court.

A court date was set, and Chris and I traveled to court together (we had only one car). We met with the judge and I explained the situation and my side of the story. I am sure Chris talked as well, but I cannot remember his justification. The judge asked him if indeed he was drinking again, and I do not remember if he denied it or not. In any case, the judge did order him to leave the house. We left the courtroom and traveled home in silence.

Chris did not leave but continued to live as if nothing had happened. So once again, I followed up with the court. This pattern was repeated three times, with Chris and me traveling to court together, listening to the judge say he needed to leave, returning home, and pretending nothing had happened! After the third time, the judge said, "You leave the house or I will put you in jail." Finally, Chris left. I do not know where he went or how long it was before the next incident. ... This was in the fall of 1985. I was pregnant again and was approximately seven months along at this time.

I knew most likely Chris would return home because he really had nowhere to go. I continued to point him in the direction of AA.

... I talked with Dalton and Sabe, who were now sixteen and eleven, and told them that if their father came home, we had the right to make him leave. In order to do so, we could call the police. I told them I was not asking them to do that but ... that we had the right.

A couple of days before Thanksgiving, as I was returning home from grocery shopping, I turned the corner to find my worst nightmare. A police car or cars were parked in the court with their flashing lights ablaze, and as I pulled into the parking space, I could see Dalton pacing back and forth in front of the townhouse. When I asked him what was going on, he said, "Dad came home and I called the police."

The policeman asked me if I had a restraining order, and I showed it to him and explained the situation.

Dalton ran to the basement, crying, and all the other boys hovered in silence, as I recall. ... I think I was in a state of shock as well, trying to deny what was happening. The police proceeded to the master bedroom, and Chris was in the bathroom taking a bath. The policemen went into the bathroom and ordered him to get dressed and come with them. After Chris left, all of us were crying. The policeman came back in, sat us all down, and explained to the boys that their Dad was sick, that he needed help and they had done the right thing by calling because now he could get the help he needed.

At this point, Chris left for the final time. He eventually found his way to AA. He lived with an AA member, and he found a job with Budget Cars and began the slow process of rebuilding his life. All of his efforts went to sustain himself. He did not have a car; he had to pay rent and buy food and he had nothing to contribute to the family.

That Christmas, I had $500 to spend on the boys. It was a bleak and terrifying time. I was alone with four sons, I was pregnant, and I was trying to work and survive. The love and help from women in Al-Anon gave me hope. The women organized a surprise baby shower for me, and members of the church were there to encourage me and help as well. I had great neighbors, the Eubanks, who invited us for Christmas Eve, and at the end of the night, [Steve Eubank] told me that if there was anything he could do to help, to please reach out to him.

Dalton commented during this time of our lives what a strange family we were. Here Chris and I were separated with me pregnant! He was sixteen years old at this time; this had to be very difficult for him!

Chris and I did stay in contact and communicated frequently. The boys and I prepared Christmas dinner and took it to him because he felt he could not come to the house at that point.

In January 1986, our fifth son (Alec) was born. It was a Friday; I had gone to work as usual, hoping that it would be ten more days before he was born on his due date. Somehow, it was easier to care for him prior to birth. I worked all day, and at 4:30 p.m., I announced to an office full of auditors that I believed the meeting was over. I called the doctor and told him that I believed I was in labor and asked if I should come to his office or go directly to the hospital. He said it was up to me. I decided to go to the doctor's office because I thought perhaps it could be a false alarm. I got in my car and drove around the

Beltway in rush hour traffic by myself while in labor! Insanity! When I arrived, the doctor checked me out and said I needed to get to the hospital immediately.

The doctor said he had to go home momentarily. He said I should call my husband and have him take me to the hospital. He said if my husband did not arrive before he returned, he would take me to the hospital. Chris came immediately and took me to the hospital.

Alec was born at 8:07 that evening. I stayed in the hospital through the weekend and came home on the Martin Luther King holiday on Monday. Chris picked Alec and me up and took us home. I vividly remember him carrying Alec into the house, laying him in his crib, coming over to me, kissing me, and then leaving. It was surreal. I thought, "What is happening to my life?" So many joys and sorrows all intertwined! I brought my computer home from work and began working that Tuesday morning, never skipping a day of work to have a baby, [just] facing life. Nuts!

While I was in the hospital, I received a call from a woman that Chris had borrowed $1,000 from. She explained what a jerk she thought he was and expressed her condolences to me, telling me how sorry she was for me. I was constantly being bombarded with bills or people trying to collect. Chris ignored all these situations, at least from my perspective. I was even sued by a neighbor because of a $15,000 investment that went bad. I went to the court by myself to defend it. Chris could never even discuss it. I have no idea what the $15,000 was even for. The neighbor eventually moved as a result of this, and they told our sons that was why they were moving. These are painful realities that are hidden deep inside that only surface years later as I am writing this epilogue.

I was constantly conflicted regarding my thoughts of Dad. I loved having him around when he was sober, but while he drank, he and Mom would constantly fight and yell. I had a lot of empathy for Dad and didn't always understand why he continued to struggle. I took it very personally, and I resented how hard Mom always was on him. That resentment engulfed me and caused me to be bitter toward my home life.

> [The month Alec was born,] Chris began to work the program at least in attending meetings. I continued to work, attend Al-Anon, live life as best I could, and take care of the boys. Chris and I lived separately and he worked, attended AA, and tried to piece some order back into his life. I was never aware of him having a sponsor, and I do not recall him mentioning any fourth-step work. However, Chris was always the one to initiate amends regarding any heat-of-the-moment conflict. He has always been the first to say "I am sorry" and try to apologize. Apologizing has never been easy for me. I always felt justified!
>
> Chris appeared to enjoy the service work, and he reached out to others in need. From my point of view, he avoided looking at himself and always compared himself out of the equation. However, the drinking did stop, and I had hope for brighter days. As I said, we never completely lost touch with each other or our relationship, so after nine months, we agreed to give our marriage a try and he moved home.
>
> During this time, we also participated in a combined AA/Al-Anon couples meeting every Saturday night. We met other couples, and for the first time in a long while, we had a little bit of social life. We had attended couple meetings for about five years when he suddenly and unexpectedly informed me that he would not be attending any more couple meetings. Shortly after that, he also quit going to AA meetings. An interesting thing that I noticed during all this was that as long as he was going to AA, he would not attempt to go to the church. I talked with the bishop about this and he told me to let it be, he would find his way. After he quit going to AA, he did begin to go to church, so I just let go of trying to understand and enjoyed my life.
>
> For the next thirteen years (1986-1999), we had some peace and happiness within the family. Chris was a very engaged father with Alec, and he was Mr. Mom a lot of the time with all of the boys. We always had dinner together as a family. During

this time, we always talked through our days and plans for the week. It was real quality time. Chris usually did the grocery shopping and the meal preparation. His work was more flexible than mine. Chris also enjoyed gardening, and he always had the most beautiful yard in the neighborhood. He had purchased a Blazer truck and he took great care of it by washing and waxing it regularly. The neighbor used to laugh and say that he was going to rub all the paint off by buffing it and polishing it off.

Temps Rising

In sixth grade, 1985-86, I started to show signs of rebellion and depression. I constantly blamed everyone else for my behavioral problems, but sitting in class and paying attention was not a strength of mine. My mother was called into the school a few times to talk about events I initiated during classes.

At the same time, I was struggling with migraines and anxiety, and the migraines were so bad I wasn't able to lie down. My head would pulse with pain, and I had to be in a totally silent, dark room to cope.

I became best friends with Jason, a kid who lived just up the street. We had many things in common, including interests in sports, girls, and living on the edge. Jason was a little older than I was, and I liked trying to keep up with him. Since we went to the same church, our families became friends as well. Outside of religion, Jason's father was a Native American. With my father being a cowboy, they seemed to click. Our moms became lifelong friends.

Jason and I would gather all the neighbor kids to play football on the golf course or to play basketball near the neighborhood pool. We also loved BMX and skateboarding. I remember getting hurt a lot playing tackle football without pads and just playing through the pain because we didn't hold back when competing with each other. We played for hours after school every day and formed a tight group of friends.

There was also a darker side to our time together. We used to find cigarettes to smoke, and some of the kids would huff butane they bought from 7-Eleven, getting high and passing out for short periods of time. I tried most of the things that the older kids would do, but huffing butane was not one of them.

Once, we heard a rumor that a kid we didn't particularly like had a stash of fireworks. His family went out of town, and five or six of us broke into their home and found the fireworks under the kid's bed. While excitedly shuffling through them, someone suggested trashing the house. We found chocolate syrup and started to squirt it everywhere, turning furniture and many other items upside down.

In that process, we found a checkbook. Tony, one of the older teens who was there with us, suggested that we go to the bank listed on the checkbook and cash the checks.

The next week, we forged a check and a few of us went to the bank. Two of us entered the bank and waited in line. When we were called up to the counter, we presented the check. We kept confident looks on our faces, but we were shocked when the lady behind the counter handed us a few hundred dollars. We repeated this two or three times. We made a pact to split the money and not talk about it.

A few months later, a policeman knocked on my door. He showed Mom a sketch from the teller that looked like a mixture of me and Tony, who had braces. Of course, we denied having anything to do with the check forging, but it was too late. Many of the kids involved told the police the details, and the police took us down to the local jail. They actually put us in a jail cell for an hour or two until they had the case all worked out.

The family didn't press charges because the mother was a Christian and forgave us. Instead, she requested that we work around her house as probation and restitution.

Another kid I became friends with was Dale. Being at his house always seemed like an escape from my home. He lived in a single-family home in a richer neighborhood called Purple Beach, and his mom would always give us tater tots and Coke after school. I envied his bigger home and that he had a mom who was there after school to fix food and cater to him. Dale's dad was the general manager of WAVA radio station, and he would give us tickets to concerts and professional sports games.

Dale and I were always chasing girls, and we both liked sports and skating. There were paved pathways all over Reston, connecting all the neighborhoods, golf courses, pools, and playgrounds. With our bikes and skateboards, we traveled all over the place.

We were mischievous as well, always looking for adventure. One day after school, we decided to start a fire in the small patch of woods in front of Dale's house. The fire ended up getting too big to control, and we had to call the fire department to put it out.

There was a little more light in our home then. Dad would help cook meals, and he kept a nice garden in the front and back of our townhome. He took to painting, something he did throughout his life whenever he was sober. There was a distinct difference when he put the bottles of vodka down and abstained—he flourished as a sensitive, kind, and gentle father.

Dad was working out at the Dulles Airport in the car rental industry, and since he was able to borrow a car from work, we had a second car. One in particular that he seemed to bring home often was a maroon Chrysler LeBaron. It had a CD player, and when you played music on it, you could skip to the next song immediately, without having to push fast-forward and wait. Music has always been an escape for me, and one day after school, Dalton and I sat in the car, put The Cars in the CD player, and jammed out. I can still picture that sunny day and the crisp sound of the CD.

Dalton was a great older brother. He set the stage for what my younger brothers and I would try to emulate when it was our turn. He was popular and seemed to do everything right, even in the midst of our family struggles. He did well in academics, became student body president of the high school, and quickly advanced as one of the school's better basketball and football players. He always wore the number 12 on the football field in honor of Roger Staubach, the Dallas Cowboys quarterback he idolized while growing up. (Being a Dallas fan in the Washington Redskins' backyard was always a conflict in neighborhood and sports conversations. We even lived near some of the Redskin players, and we would flaunt our Cowboy gear.)

I loved going to Dalton's games, either basketball or football, and felt proud that he was my older brother. We younger boys used that pride in our own practice, on game days, and even on the blacktops or makeshift fields where we played with friends.

I remember having four priorities during seventh and eighth grade: girls, friends, football, and basketball. They were all interwoven and gave me an outlet. My mother, who always seemed to be pushing me on many fronts, tried to balance my activities with church and Boy Scouts. My brothers and I also took piano lessons and had to practice every day after school. I enjoyed piano when I could play the songs I was interested in and not what the teacher wanted me to play.

One of the most sacred things my mother did for us every day was to cook a hot meal before school and read to us from the scriptures while we ate. It was early in the morning, and I imagine our attitudes were not the best, but she did it every day before she went to work throughout my entire childhood and teenage life. She knew what needed to be done to raise boys into men.

She always had change for us to take to school for lunch, and she made dinner for us every night from what seemed to be an empty kitchen. She cooked from ingredients and sacrificed her time after long days at work to help us with homework, Scouts, and shuffling to sports activities. Dad did help, but it was my mom's constant schedule that I remember the most.

> Chris had a steady job with consecutive car rental companies: Budget, Dollar, and then Bargain Buggies. During this time, we had a complimentary car, and usually gas was included. However, eventually, he left that business. He claims I pressured him too much to climb the corporate ladder and that nothing was ever good enough for me. … He then began to pursue starting his own car rental business, and he also put a down payment down on two vans for the shuttle business. I began to be fearful again that we were headed for another merry-go-round.
>
> I do not recall how many years he worked with the car rental business, but they are considered some of the better years we have had financially. From the car rental companies, he floundered between non-employment, True Green, and eventually baggage handling for United Airlines. He worked for United for probably about four or five years. He eventually quit there and delivered baggage for a short period of time.
>
> During this span of time, we focused on raising our sons. We supported them in their academics and tried to really create a stable home for them. Chris was very encouraging and supportive of their sports, especially football. We had a starting quarterback at the local high school for eleven consecutive years as we watched each [of our sons assume] that position. We spent a lot of time in the fall going to four games a week. We enjoyed these family activities, and I have many fond memories of the cool crisp fall evenings spent out of doors. Chris also coached several basketball teams during these years, both the church team and local community leagues. The boys' friends always

enjoyed Chris, and he had an interest in all their lives.

Also during these years, Chris participated in church and church activities. He has never really been what you could consider "active" of his own accord, but he would attend, sitting in the back row and always on the periphery. He would laugh and say what a good bad example he was. He did not take the church callings[1] that were offered to him, and he did not like having home teachers[2] come to the house. However, when Dalton returned from his mission[3] in 1992, we were sealed as a family in the Washington D.C. Temple.[4] That was a happy day in my life. It was something I had yearned and longed for, the ideal I strived for, and at last, I felt the journey had been worth it.

All of our sons achieved Eagle Scout rank, and Chris was supportive of those achievements. He even provided some of the leadership in the Scouting organization during those years. All five sons graduated from four years of early morning seminary.[5] ... Chris was supportive of all these activities as well, but I was the one who always took the lead and did the majority of the work to make it happen.

During this time, I was the major breadwinner and I always managed the family finances and provided the funding for the [boys'church] missions and college.

... Chris spent many hours developing his artistic talent, and he painted feverishly. He was very prolific and produced many wonderful oil paintings and some watercolors. Many, he

---

1. Volunteer positions within the Church of Jesus Christ of Latter-day Saints.
2. Men assigned to assist a specific family within the Church of Jesus Christ. This program has been discontinued.
3. In the Church of Jesus Christ, all males are asked to perform six to twenty-four months of proselytizing, humanitarian, or other services for the church. This is called a "mission." At this time, the earliest a young man could begin a mission was age nineteen. Girls are invited to serve, as well, but it is not considered a duty for them to do so, like it is for boys.
4. In the Church of Jesus Christ, a "sealing ordinance" is when a couple's marriage is blessed to continue for eternity, meaning that the couple is still married after death. This ordinance is only performed in Church of Jesus Christ of Latter-day Saint temples, and to be eligible, both husband and wife must be living in accordance with the gospel as taught by the church.

> gave as gifts, and we have many more displayed in our home currently. These have been a source of joy for him and also for the family. Many friends also admire his artwork, and he has actually sold some of it.

During middle school, I played on the A teams for football and on the AAU basketball team each year after playing with the top travel teams for my age. I struggled in school academically, but playing on the football and basketball teams and having many friends gave me something to look forward to. In eighth grade, I was named "most athletic" for the school. I was one of the bigger kids on the football team, and coaches would put me in on the line or as linebacker. I wanted to run the ball, but the coaches' sons always seemed to have those spots.

After school, if there weren't organized sports to go to, I spent most of my time hanging out with girls or playing basketball on the courts around the school. I was always dating older girls. One in particular was Haley. She was one of the popular girls in the grade above me, and we would talk all night on the phone, go to movies together, and hang out after school. I was always intimidated by her and wondered why she liked me.

Two Personas

A few weeks before my freshman year started, I found myself trying out for the freshman football team. I was excited to be in high school and trying out for the team; Dalton had been quarterback for the varsity team for a couple of years and was now on the football team at BYU. The coaches asked me to try out for QB, but I was reluctant because I wanted to play running back and linebacker and I would be going up against very good competition that year, kids who seemed a lot more experienced and bigger than me. Besides, I had never played QB. The only experience I had playing QB was on the golf course with all the neighborhood kids.

As we progressed through that first week of freshman football practice, I threw the ball well and connected with the receivers running their patterns. I can remember being surprised that I could throw a spiral as tight as I could. As the receivers ran their routes, I was able to lead them with the ball perfectly. Subsequently, I earned the position of starting QB for the first game.

We swept teams all season because we had a complete team, both offensively and defensively. We could run the ball well, and our passing game exceeded my expectations. Our standout player that year was Dean Matyja, an oversized running back who ran faster than anyone who stepped on the field. He had never played football on an organized team and had to learn the concepts of the plays and how to run and hold the ball properly, but it didn't matter—he could outrun everyone and scored two or three touchdowns a game. We ended the season undefeated.

Coach Bruderer, the varsity coach, came to a few of our games and asked some of us to dress for varsity at the end of the season. It was a surreal time in my life: I was a freshman dressing on varsity after playing

QB for the first time. I felt honored.

That summer, I worked hard to make the varsity team, which I did at the start of the season. That meant I was going to be playing with and against seniors when I was only fifteen years old, 5'10", and about 160 pounds.

I was the second-string QB backing the senior starter, Glenn. After we ended the hot summer practices, our first game was against T.C. Williams, which had always been one the best teams in the area and in the nation.[1] I remember everyone being hyped and nervous to play such a good team for our first game.

As the game got started, T.C. Williams racked up points. It became very apparent that they were much better than us. Glenn was eventually pulled from play due to injury and poor performance, and the coaches called my name and told me that I would be going in. It was raining, and the field had turned into a mud bowl. Until I was tackled into the mud, I was the only clean jersey for a few plays.

Calling the plays as a sophomore in my first live varsity game, and particularly in a game with such high-quality players, made me feel nervous and on edge. Playing QB can be very nerve-racking because you handle the ball for every play and every call, step, and throw can make a big impact on the game. On top of that, T.C. Williams had giants with full-blown beards. But play after play, my confidence grew. We didn't pass much because of the rain, but I was able to take care of the ball and run the offense as best as I could under the circumstances.

The only good that came from that game was that I won the starting varsity position. Not only did I win the position of QB as a sophomore, but I hooked up with Jerika, one of the sophomore cheerleaders. She was new to the school, and many of the older kids were interested in her, including Glenn.

Tensions were high in the locker room that week in practice. One day, Glenn confronted me and punched me in the chest. He was taller and bigger than me and good friends with all our older teammates. It was a very awkward position to be in; however, a few of our teammates broke up the confrontation. They seemed to embrace me, and we moved on.

That wasn't the only time that I was helped in a fight by my teammates. I once got in a fight with a "punk" senior and he jumped me in the hallway. I took control of the fight and got the best of him, and he ended up being

---

1. In 2000, Hollywood made a movie about this team. It was called *Remember the Titans*.

suspended. He wasn't happy about getting suspended, and he wasn't happy that I got the advantage over him instead of backing down. One weekend, he and a few of his friends went looking for me at a party where some of the football players were. He asked where I was, and our star running back, Jake, led him to a back bedroom in the house. As they went to that particular room, Jake, who was the strongest player on the team, jumped the senior and his friends. He beat them so bad that the kid ended up in the hospital with a broken jaw that had to be wired shut.

I remember my classmates getting in a lot of fights on the weekends or at school. There were drugs and guns at school, and who you hung out with dictated the kind of trouble you got into.

One day in school, Damont, who I knew from football, came up to me in the hallway, pushed me against the wall, and put a gun to my chest as a joke. It was a little .22 pistol, and he wanted to show me his firepower. On other occasions, a few of my friends from the team would show off the hundreds of dollars they had in their pockets from selling drugs in the school. Never personally having had more than what I needed for lunch, I got tired of seeing cash. Once, as one of my old freshman teammates Jorge handed me a handful of cash to hold, I purposely dropped a $20 on the floor and stepped on it. If he had found out, he would have had me jumped and beaten badly. Sadly, he lost his life the following year. No one wanted to talk about it, but he was hanging around the wrong crowd and was shot.

In my sophomore year, I was in the school's Mr. Seahawk pageant. Each year, guys were crowned for having the best talent, best style, and best appearance. Things were still tight at home, financially, and I remember not having a lot of clothes that I really liked. As the show approached, I was at a local clothing shop and they asked me if I would model their clothing in the Mr. Seahawk show. In exchange, they would let me keep the clothing. I was very excited and gladly accepted.

For my talent piece in the pageant, I played the *Pink Panther* theme on the piano. Before that, no one at school knew that I even played the piano. I had it memorized and impressed everyone. I won best talent but didn't win the overall Mr. Seahawk title.

As a QB, I seemed to attract the attention of more girls. I also began to experiment with alcohol despite my father trying to be sober. My first long-term relationship was with Rachel, one of the captains of the cheerleading squad. We dated on and off for over two years. She was the first girl I said

I loved. I wanted to be with her every day after school, and we spent a lot of time together on the weekends.

One school night while I was at her house, I lied to my parents about where I was because they wouldn't have approved of me being with her so late. After midnight, I finally made the trek home on my bike. I had to come up with a lie that would satisfy my parents, so on the way, I scratched up my bike, messed up my hair, and scratched my arm until it bled. I walked in the door crying and told my parents I had been struck by a car in a hit and run. They were shocked and told me to go to bed and get some rest. The next day, they called the police.

When the police arrived, I had to give them my fabricated story. They suggested taking me to the hospital to get checked, so we went to the hospital and the lie continued. It kept getting deeper and more entangled as I repeated the story of being struck by a car and left on the roadside. The doctor said I had a concussion and instructed my parents to keep me home from school for a few days. They did, and I got away with the lie.

To this day, I still scratch my head as to why the doctor diagnosed a concussion.

I wasn't the best boyfriend, so my relationship with Rachel was turbulent. I was obsessed with spending time with her, and I was very jealous and often questioned what she wore to school. She sometimes wore jean overalls that were revealing and drove me crazy, and I couldn't deal with the fact that other guys were looking at her.

There were questions of cheating on both sides (mostly mine) right from the start. I wasn't true to her, and my emotions and obsession with her were both tainted by my infidelity. I had little trust both ways.

Drinking, smoking weed, and the beginnings of anxiety and depression during that time didn't help, either.

One day while hanging with some of my friends, I compiled a list of all the girls I had hooked up with during the time I'd been dating Rachel. For some stupid reason, I kept that note in my top dresser drawer, where Rachel found it. I'm sure it was devastating for her to read. A few of her friends and fellow cheerleaders were on that list, as well as other girls she knew from the school. Additionally, I would go on vacation to Utah with my family every summer to see cousins, and we always seemed to find girls and party. After Rachel found that note in my dresser, she and a few of her closest friends confronted me at a party and some of them started punching me. I took the blows as the cheater in the relationship, only raising my arms to protect my face and head. They cut my lip and chipped my tooth. I deserved it.

I had two personas emerging at the same time: I was the guy who participated in church every week, attended seminary before school, played football as the varsity QB, and earned an Eagle Scout rank. But there was also a dark side of me that involved alcohol, weed, partying, and hooking up with girls. Not many people saw that side of me. Most only paid attention to my successes, and my dark side seemed to go unnoticed.

Mom started to restrict my privileges because I would stay out late or have a bad attitude. I remember always being mad at her for only allowing me to go out for one night each weekend. I would stay in my room and punch my head or hit it against the wall in anger.

I had a lot of anger and felt insecure and conflicted about all my lies, cheating, and success. I also suffered from migraines, lack of sleep, and constant stress over academics. I had ADD but was never diagnosed or given treatment. Instead, I learned to manipulate, to deflect, and to use my position in school athletics to convince teachers and counselors to do what I wanted.

All my successes and failures came to a head in my senior year.

We had one of the best football teams in school history and were a state contender in the highest conference in Virginia. Many of the seniors had played varsity for three years, and we gelled as a solid team that had playoff hopes.

As the season started, we were all very excited to repeat the undefeated year we had had as freshmen. We won our first two games and were ranked in all the newspapers. However, that came to halt after a few key players, including me, sustained injuries in the third week. My injury happened during practice: A teammate was too aggressive when he grabbed my arm, and it caused a small tear in my shoulder. The doctor suggested I get surgery, which would mean ending my senior season. I thought about it and decided to sit out two games and see how I was feeling with no surgery.

Unfortunately, we lost those two games. Those two losses were terribly disappointing, and I wanted to get back in and help save our senior year. I decided to forgo surgery and play injured and asked our medical trainer to wrap up my shoulder for all remaining games that year. With other players coming off injuries and my shoulder wrapped, we went on winning the rest of our games during the regular season and topped the polls in all the newspapers.

My shoulder hurt all year long and I was restricted in my throwing ability, but we were able to advance and win the regional finals against Robinson High School, one of the biggest programs in Virginia. The following week, we drove down to Halifax, Virginia, and played the best team in the state. I was sacked seven times that day, more than the entire season combined. During halftime, Coach Bruderer rallied us by playing "In the Air" by Phil Collins. We made a surge on the last drive of the game and scored, but it was too little, too late. Halifax won the state finals that year. We were still proud of what we had accomplished and learned that year, and I was excited about possibly playing in college.

After my senior year, I was awarded 3rd Team All-State, WUSA Channel 9 All-Met, and All-Region. To this day, I am still on the list of the most all-time throwing yards and completions in Virginia history. It was something to be proud of.

So much for my successes. By my senior year, I had burned a lot of relationships and was dating girls from other schools. During parties, I expressed arrogance and extreme outbursts of aggression. Drugs and alcohol became a weekend staple. I was involved in a lot of fights and would intimidate anyone who questioned me or my behaviors, even close friends. I didn't want to be at school and left each day at noon to work at a technology firm shipping mainframe computers. I was fascinated by all the components and inner workings of computers, and I enjoyed getting off school property, earning money for my bad habits, and having the latest shoes and clothes. Besides that, making money worked better for me than sitting in class.

One particular night near the end of my senior year, I was at a girl's house and we decided to get into her jacuzzi. We found some grain liquor in her home and began to take shots. The jacuzzi intensified my buzz, and I reached an all-time high that I had never experienced before.

After midnight, I drove home drunk, as I had done many nights. Once there, I snuck up to my room. Our townhouse consisted of six split-level floors, and my bedroom was on the top floor. On my way up, I woke my father. He came into my room and, since I smelled like alcohol and had my pants on backward, confronted me. I'm not sure who started it, but we began to wrestle and I started throwing punches. We fought and wrestled while falling down three flights of stairs. Once I got loose from his grip, I started punching holes in the walls and threatening to grab the shotgun we kept in the house.

As my father and I continued to fight, my mother called the police.

When they arrived, I started fighting them, too. I grabbed one of their baton sticks and was winning the battle, but more police officers showed up and started to pound me with their sticks. At one point, I was standing on a couch, kicking them as they approached, until they overcame me with brutal force and held me down. They eventually twisted me into a straitjacket and tied me to a longboard. I was sent off in an ambulance while threatening the paramedics that I would take my life.

After going to the hospital, I was placed in a white padded room in the Fairfax Ward, still in a straitjacket to keep me from harming myself.

> ... Sabe has given us a lot of grief through the years, and in one incident, we had to call the police and have him straitjacketed. Chris was the one who asked me to call the police because Sabe was punching and throwing his fists at him. They put him into a mental hospital for several days. Sabe was very embarrassed by this situation, and I was terrified. I envisioned his life, following the footsteps of his father, and I demanded some counseling with the whole family at that time.

The beating I had endured from the police was so intense that as I looked in the mirror in the bathroom the next day, I couldn't recognize my face.

No one pressed charges, and I ended up staying in the hospital for a week. I was not put on medicine or diagnosed with anything. Instead, the incident was quickly forgotten and not discussed—swept under the rug, if you will. I continued going to school through the end of my senior year, including going to prom and senior week.

College: A New Leaf

I had received letters of interest from Brigham Young University (BYU), Penn State, East Carolina, Vanderbilt, and several Division II and III colleges leading up to my senior year. However, due to poor grades, my torn shoulder, and being a little undersized, all the colleges that had expressed interest in me previously dried up. So instead, I went to play football at Ricks College, an Idaho junior college and feeder school for BYU.

One of the big reasons I chose to attend Ricks College was that it was a church college and I thought I could try to turn my life around there. At that time, boys in our church were asked to serve a two-year proselytizing mission when they were nineteen years old, and each prospective missionary was required to be clean from major sin for at least one year before going. I had witnessed the benefits that Dalton received from serving a mission in California a few years earlier, and after my volatile senior year, I knew if I didn't clean up my life, I wouldn't be able to follow his example. I had to be sober and celibate for a year to have any chance.

I reported for football a few weeks before school started, and my parents dropped me off at a house where many of the older football players were also staying. It was a mile or so off campus. There were seven or eight bedrooms, and I remember being somewhat excited. I say "somewhat" because my shoulder was still bugging me and I hadn't been able to put in the training that I was accustomed to each summer. My bad behavior and depression also continued to affect me. I felt like a ticking time bomb. I acquired a pistol that summer and had a bag of marijuana in my suitcase when I was dropped off. As my parents left to go back home, I felt somewhat lost and conflicted.

My first week at Ricks College was full of parties, drugs, and alcohol. We attended the two dance clubs in Rexburg, drove out to the sand dunes, and partied in the house.

The first day of football was a disaster. The quarterbacks were separated from the other players, and as we began to warm up and put our throwing capabilities on display for the coaches, I felt a sharp pain in my shoulder again. This time, I didn't have an athletic trainer wrap my shoulder. I just tried to deal with the pain and discomfort as the day went on.

I remember feeling disconnected when all the players came into a circle and did the usual yelling and chanting. With the parties and drug abuse, my hurt shoulder, depression, and just not feeling football anymore, I decided to walk off the field and never return again.

I spent the rest of that week in my room, in a deep depression. Then, right as school was starting, a group of us were called into the dean's office for having alcohol and marijuana and staying overnight at the sand dunes with girls, which was against the school's honor code. We all sat through a disciplinary council and had to describe the events that had taken place that night. I remember having to draw how each of us had been sitting in the car on a chalkboard and recounting how a joint was passed around. I drew some crazy zig-zag lines, noting that it skipped over me when it hadn't, in reality.

One of the kids who had been with me was a roommate of mine, a very good friend from high school and a star athlete. He and I were dating girls who lived together. Ricks College had curfews and many rules, all of which we disobeyed from the very beginning. Simply put, I was not ready to be at a church college. We were both put on probation after the disciplinary council, and he ended up getting kicked out of the school. He covered for me that day so that I wouldn't be.

I was at a very low point. I tried attending college classes at the beginning but got more involved with the girl I was dating and found it a pain to bike all the way to class every day. I had already disappointed everyone back home by quitting football, and my life was spiraling out of control with self-medication and depression.

I decided to turn myself in and scheduled a time to talk with the bishop of my congregation. He seemed to like football players, and I trusted him. There was a lot that I had to confess, and it wasn't going to be easy. I was very nervous the day of the appointment and remember during the interview that the bishop was very understanding and listened as I poured out all the immorality and all the self-medication that I had gotten myself into. I wasn't able to take the sacrament for a time and had to meet often with the bishop over the next several weeks. I vowed to Christ, the bishop, and myself that I wouldn't drink, smoke, or be immoral from that point on. The girl I was dating was the Relief Society president[1] in her ward[2]. Her being such a good girl helped me push myself in the new life that I wanted to build. As we dated, I found it easy to stay away from alcohol and weed, but only kissing her was a struggle because we were very attracted to each other.

I seemed to get into a lot of fights with her, and looking back, I was in a rabbit hole of depression. I often stayed in my room and missed classes. Once, I found a local store that had glow-in-the-dark paint, and while I was home and my roommates were all at school, I painted a mountain scene on all the walls, with stars on the ceiling. You could see it when the room was dark, and I was pretty proud of it.

As we came to the end of the fall semester, I had a 1.9 GPA and it was apparent that I did not want to attend school the next semester. I wanted to go home and get ready to serve a mission. My girlfriend and I decided to break up because I was leaving and she wanted to date men who were already home from their missions so she could marry within the next year or two.

Right before I left to go home for Christmas break, I met a few girls I went on dates with. One was a friend of my ex-girlfriend's. I was abstaining from immorality, drinking, and smoking, and she knew that. One night, we decided to go back to my place. As the night went on, we ended up in my bedroom. I was sitting on my bed, and she told me to close my eyes. Once I had, she undressed into her matching Victoria Secret underwear and then jumped on me. The temptation was so apparent that I stood up, turned her around, placed her on the bed, and stopped the situation from continuing.

Once I returned home to Virginia, I spent the next six months preparing to serve a mission. I read several books, including the scriptures, and started to learn and understand more about what Jesus Christ did for me and the human race. I started to understand myself more and felt guilt

---

1. The Relief Society is the women's organization of the Church of Jesus Christ of Latter-day Saints.
2. A single congregation.

for all the sins I had committed. My depressive episodes started to become fewer and further apart the more I submerged myself in getting ready for a mission and abstaining from bad behavior.

I submitted a mission application to the church's headquarters, and weeks later, I received my assignment. As I opened the letter, I was surprised to read that I would be serving in Sao Paulo, Brazil. At first, I thought that meant I would be speaking Spanish, but later in the letter, it said that Portuguese was the official language.

That summer was a blast. I spent time hanging out with my best friends from church and school. The places we frequented and the things we did were wholesome and drama-free.

I met a girl I was very fond of who went to a neighboring high school. As usual, I fell hard and fast for her, and we spent a lot of time together leading up to my mission.

As the start of my mission approached, I said my goodbyes to everyone. I felt both excited and nervous thinking that I would be living in a foreign country for two years. Because of all the books I had read, I also felt ready. My behavior had improved, and my choices were reflective of that. I had a desire to learn Portuguese and teach the principles that my mother had tried to instill in me as a youth. Memories of her reading scriptures to us every morning before school and dragging us to church every Sunday, which must have been a true sacrifice and struggle, began to surface with appreciation and gratitude. I had a new lease on life and felt free of the drugs, alcohol, and immorality that had plagued me. I wanted to spread the message of freedom and repentance I had experienced firsthand.

The hardest goodbye, besides to my family, was to the girl I was seeing. One of the rules of a mission then was that missionaries were not allowed to call anyone outside of their assignment except for family, and even family calls were only allowed on Mother's Day and Christmas. This girl was not a member of the Church of Jesus Christ and didn't quite understand why I had volunteered to go on a mission and would only be contacting her through letters for two years. But we promised to write to each other, and the last day I saw her, I brought roses and said my goodbyes. There were a lot of tears. I badly wanted her to wait for me to return from Sao Paulo so we could see where things would go.

Missionary Life

I spent the first ninety days of my mission in Provo, Utah, in the Missionary Training Center (MTC). My stay there was initially only supposed to be for eight weeks, but visa problems kept me in the States.

When I first arrived at the MTC, my parents and I were shuffled into a room full of parents and newly appointed missionaries to learn what was ahead of us in the MTC and to say our last goodbyes. Each missionary was then assigned another missionary to be our companion, or partner, for the period of time we would spend in the MTC. I became Elder Anderson and was assigned to a companion from Utah, Elder Morgan.

We immediately began classes and forged ahead in learning Portuguese. My brief studies in Spanish and French in high school assisted with that, and I picked up the language quickly. I also memorized and role-played the lessons I would be teaching in Brazil. For the first time, I felt energized and enlightened instead of depressed.

Our days consisted of classes, meals, and the occasional recreational time and assemblies. I met many great future leaders and young men who put their lives on hold for two years to serve and further the work of the gospel.

As Elder Morgan and I approached our last month in the MTC, we were both asked to be assistants to the president (APs), helping teach and lead new missionaries as they entered the MTC. It was an honor to be an AP and to serve with Elder Morgan.

Since my final month in the MTC had not been planned, my companion and I had to make our own schedule of study and recreation. It was hard, but we were able to attend the temple almost daily, which became a great experience and helped me feel close to the Spirit. We learned about the plan of salvation, Joseph Smith's conversion and story, the scriptures, and all the lessons that we would be teaching investigators in Brazil.

When we finally received our visas, we left, ready to hit the streets of Brazil. There were twelve of us headed to Sao Paulo, and as our plane began to descend, I remember looking out of the window and being overwhelmed at the size of the city. It looked ten times larger than New York City. As the plane got closer, I could see some of the poorer suburbs. I saw tin roofs on cinder block walls. Many of the homes were made of plywood over dirt floors. My anxieties grew as the reality hit me: I was entering a completely foreign land, without my family and friends, and would soon have to be knocking on doors, conversing in these people's native tongue, for what seemed to be a very long time.

We were hustled from the airport to the mission office in Santo Amaro, Brazil, where there were mattresses on the floor for arriving missionaries. We quickly dropped off our bags and were shuffled off to meet Interim Mission President Sousa.

We had heard that many of the missionaries in the Sao Paulo mission disobeyed mission rules. President Sousa, a native Brazilian, had been cleaning the mission up and sent over thirty missionaries home early.

When it was my turn to meet with the president, I entered his office and he sat me down and made me feel welcome. He related the story of his conversion to the gospel and told me that the mission was being rebuilt and needed leadership. He warned me that my first companion was close to being kicked out because of his behavior. However, this missionary only had a short time to go before he completed his two years, and President Sousa wanted to give him the chance to complete his mission.

After a few days of training in the mission office, we were bused to our new areas and companions. My first home consisted of one main room and a small bathroom. The main room had a stove and two bunk beds, and since four of us were staying there, two of us slept on the concrete floor until we bought extra beds. The house was surrounded by a wall with broken glass cemented to its top to keep burglars out.

My companion was from Brazil and was goofing off from the get-go, testing me on which rules I would keep. There were pictures of Madonna on our walls, and he was a very dynamic person who had the other missionaries in our apartment manipulated into bending the rules. When we visited people, he would often overstay our welcome and participate in activities or conversations that seemed like a waste of time.

I wasn't on a mission to goof off; I had spent many years doing that already and knew it was a dead end. If I was going to be in a foreign land serving God, I was going to obey the rules. I also made a goal of never speaking English while in Brazil.

I would wake up an hour earlier than I had to, go into the bathroom, sit on the toilet, and study the scriptures and the language. There were also many days when I stayed in our apartment by myself (against mission rules) because my companion wanted to leave our assigned area and go to the mall or somewhere we weren't allowed (a worse infraction).

The work is hard enough, but when you don't obey the rules or work hard, the guilt will eat you up, making it impossible to be so far from home. Sleeping on the concrete floor and dealing with my companion made for a very hard time adjusting to my new life. However, I stood my ground, kept the rules, and quickly picked up the language.

Eventually, additional beds arrived and my companion left for home. I received an awesome second companion, someone who had just served as the president's assistant. He too would go home soon, but it was a breath of fresh air to get a companion who knew and respected the Lord's work. We knocked on doors, talked to people in the streets, and finally found families to teach. The work was fulfilling. I truly welcomed having an obedient companion.

One particular Sunday, a sign-up sheet was passed around for members of the congregation to volunteer to feed us lunch. Afterward, a small older lady walked up to us and indicated that she had signed up to feed us that week. She described where she lived in great detail, not only telling us the bus route but also her address coordinates.

A few days passed, and on the day that the sweet sister from church was going to feed us, we hurried to the bus stop and headed out. It was a 45- to 60-minute bus ride. As time passed, the people and homes became more sparse. Soon, we felt as if we were in the jungle. Homes were buried in the thickness of the green foliage, and we could only see trees.

The bus approached the stop that the woman had described so elaborately during church. We stepped off the bus and reached for the address, then began to panic: We had forgotten to grab the piece of paper that contained her address. Another bus wouldn't pass for some time, and we could see only a few long roads and even fewer homes. There wasn't anyone around to ask for directions. We were in the middle of the jungle and alone.

Already running a bit late, we walked up and down many roads, trying to see if anything was familiar. Not only was it not familiar, but the addresses were not in order (which is very common in Brazil). Every road we walked only seemed to confuse us. We knew that this woman had sacrificed to prepare a grand meal and feed extra mouths. Hope was fading fast.

Just when all seemed lost, a thought came to my mind. I asked my companion, "Do you have faith?"

He said, "Of course I do. Why?"

I said, "Let's say a prayer and ask Heavenly Father to show us her address with the Book of Mormon." He asked how, and I responded by saying that whatever chapter number we opened to would be her house number.

After saying a prayer and asking to be guided to this sister, I blindly opened the Book of Mormon and landed on Alma 50.[1] With faith, hope, and a number but no road name, we set off to find a house with the number 50. We walked up and down more streets, searching for 50, and came upon a house that had a little sign with the number 25 on it right above a piece of paper pinned to the post with an even larger number 25 written on it. We said, "This must be it. 25 plus 25 is 50."

The home was set back in the woods, and a little path led to it from the address post. Hoping, we clapped our hands to call for her, as is customary in Brazil. It was late, and I'm sure she had given up and we had disappointed her. But when she heard our clapping, she came running and welcomed us with open arms. She had prepared a wonderful meal and even offered one of her chickens as a gesture of her love of the church and missionary work.

We didn't speak much during lunch; we were hungry and kind of in shock at what had just transpired. As we closed the meal, we asked if we could share a message with her. Since I was still new to Brazil and learning the language, it was my senior companion who told her about the miracle that had just occurred.

Little did we know that she also had a message and miracle that made the whole thing possible. After we told our side of the story, of faith, hope, and the power of the Book of Mormon, she shared that she had felt inspired to make another, bigger sign that read "25" so that we could see it. What seemed so small—lunch—had become significant to all of us. That

---

1. The Book of Alma in the Book of Mormon is the only book with over fifty chapters.

experience set the tone for the rest of my mission.

We taught lessons in that area and performed a lot of service, and it felt great. I received letters from friends and family, and they kept my spirits high. I carried a dictionary around and used every spare moment I had to memorize words, so my Portuguese was progressing nicely. My goal of never speaking English while in Brazil was still in practice, and many of the locals thought I was a German immigrant from the southern part of Brazil, where there is a high density of Germans.

As the weeks and months passed, I had many experiences serving and teaching families about Christ. I moved to a few more areas and was paired with different companions. I had the privilege of baptizing many families and individuals on a monthly and sometimes weekly basis.

Leaving My Mission

After a year of being out on the mission, I was transferred to a new area. While we were in the streets finding and talking to people interested in hearing our message, I stumbled upon a few individuals who lived in a new apartment complex in a very densely populated, wooded area that offered affordable housing. It was not close to our home, and it was a few miles' walk from the nearest bus stop, so my companion and I moved to a house closer to that complex. After that, we made the trek to the complex through the woods each day.

It seemed like people were interested in talking to us at every door we knocked on in that area. At night, which was when families were home, we had lessons every thirty minutes. The lessons were stacked so closely together that we had to shorten our messages and write down the people's questions to be answered later. I also had to come up with a way to organize all their interests and document who was who. At one point, I wrote to the mission president and asked him to send another set of missionaries to help with the work.

As soon as we began to see success, we also began to have a lot of strange things happen to us. Many times while walking back home in the woods at night, we would hear and see people practicing black magic rituals. One night, we came upon a group of people dressed in all white. They were singing and dancing around a bowl with a dead chicken in it and marking themselves with its blood.

On another occasion, we had just come out of the woods and onto the cement when two individuals across the street started yelling at us, saying, "Where are your arms?", meaning our protection.

I had a very strong feeling come over me that I needed to be brave and poised. My companion had been robbed at gunpoint while out teaching with another missionary just a few weeks before, so I had to be ready for the worst. I yelled back at them, "Here are our arms/protection," and held up the Book of Mormon and Bible.

They began to approach us, and I had a very dark feeling come over me. I could see that my companion was very nervous and wanted to run. The two men were very aggressive in their tone and language, and I had an overwhelming feeling that they were not of this world. I had been taught at some point that if you come upon evil spirits, you should put your hand out and try to shake theirs. They wouldn't shake my hand, so I turned to my companion and told him to turn around and walk with me. I knew they couldn't do anything to us and that we would be protected.

After we had reached a little distance, my companion wasn't well, so I told him to turn around and look. When we did, we saw that the men had disappeared. It was as if they had never been there. That experience was a reminder to me of the forces that were fighting the Lord's work.

This area meant a lot to me, and I was very proud of the work we were doing. I met many great families and people. One little boy, a nine- or ten-year-old kid we saw playing soccer every day, stood out to me the most. We eventually asked if we could play soccer with him. He had a makeshift ball, and playing with him became routine each time we entered the little complex surrounded by jungle. We learned that this young boy only studied for four hours a day, including lunch and recess (soccer). He lived alone with his mom, who worked many jobs and didn't get home until late each night, and he wasn't allowed into his home until his mother returned because their belongings were safer behind locked doors. So for the rest of the day, he took care of himself, eating very little food and doing few constructive activities. His situation reminded me of my own hardworking mother, who had tried to keep us busy with sports after school. He was sad to not have a father in his life, so we taught him about our Father in Heaven. I often wonder about how this young boy turned out. I hope he remembers my white shirt, tie, and black badge and the messages we shared with him.

I started having a lot of migraines. Migraines had plagued me since I was twelve years old, but these were more frequent and were coupled with fevers and stomach issues. Many days, I had to rest and our work was interrupted. My companion was annoyed with me because I wanted to stay in and he had to do splits (trade companions for a short time) with other missionaries on the days I was sick.

Around this time, I received a letter from my girlfriend back home saying that she wasn't interested in my belief system, nor did she want to continue writing or pursuing a possible relationship after my mission.

Between that letter and continually being sick, I began to feel disconnected and frustrated. I lost a lot of weight, and my mission president had me live in his house while I went to doctor appointments to figure out what was wrong with me. At one point, I had to stay in temple housing on the temple grounds by myself. It was the longest week of my life. I was miserable; my mission seemed to be slipping away from me at the height of the work and my progression as a missionary. I was losing hope and motivation to fight what was going on with me, and I remember having the thought that I wanted to go outside and find a girl to kiss so that I could get kicked out of the mission.

I dealt with the migraines and sickness for about a month before finally asking my mission president to send me home. I remember him going to a quiet room and saying a prayer to ask Heavenly Father if he should send me home. When he came back down the hallway, I remember him being very concerned and loving but saying he felt strongly that I should stay on the mission. I took that advice for a day or two but just couldn't deal with not having my own answer to what was wrong with me. I again asked to be sent home, and he agreed this time. He booked a flight, and within a week, I was sent home.

Upon returning home, I received an honorable release from the headquarters of the church. I felt like a failure for only serving fourteen months of my two-year mission.

I continued to go to doctors and found out that I had a high number of parasites in my stool. With the eradication of the parasites in my system and getting rest from the stressful life of a missionary, I was able to heal.

After two months, I really wanted to go back on a mission. I asked the leadership of our local area if I could be sent out again, and my second mission call came a few weeks later. I was called to serve in a Portuguese-speaking area of the Hartford, Connecticut, mission for the time that remained from my original mission. I remember feeling overwhelmed before leaving; this time, I knew how hard the daily life of a missionary was and I was nervous about whether I could rise to the occasion again.

I said my goodbyes again and we drove to Dulles airport. I had an empty feeling inside and felt sad and overwhelmed. When it came time to board the small commuter airline heading to Hartford, there was only one other passenger on the flight. When we reached 30,000 feet, the flight attendants asked if we were okay and then went to their stations and relaxed for the entire flight. I felt very alone, and I began to imagine the plane crashing.

When we landed, I met my new mission president and his wife. They were excited to have a missionary who was already fluent in Portuguese. They paired me with a companion and put me in Pawtucket, Rhode Island.

My new companion was a very interesting dude—strange, at best. He showed me his collection of heavy metal music (which is not allowed on the mission), and he had a picture of the mission president's wife on his wall that he would throw darts at. He wasn't at all interested in waking up on time and was hesitant about the work. I threw myself back into it as best I could, waking up at 6:30 a.m. and studying by myself until my companion would wake up.

Many of the individuals who spoke Portuguese in that area were from Cape Verde. Their dialect of Portuguese was different, but within the first couple of weeks, I was able to manage.

One early morning three or four weeks after I arrived, I awkwardly kinked my neck while doing push-ups. I was in a lot of pain and had to lie down. I wasn't able to work that day, and when the pain didn't go away after a few days, I decided to call the mission president to see if I should go to the doctor. He agreed and took me to a doctor, who prescribed a muscle relaxant. Afterward, the mission president had me stay the night at his home.

That night, I had a migraine. I mentioned it to the president's wife, who also suffered from migraines, and she offered me one of her medications. When I went to bed, the combined medications made me feel high, and my old inclinations and sexual impulses came back. I reverted back to satisfying that impulse.

It had been over two years since I had last done that, and I felt immensely ashamed. I was racked with thoughts of failure, and the high I was on intensified those feelings. Total despair came over me. I wanted to end my life. I looked over at the bottle of pills on the counter and decided to ingest all of them.

After I swallowed the bottle of pills, I started sweating profusely. I put on my T-shirt, jeans, and shoes (without socks) and headed out into the cold winter night. Once outside, I ran down the empty road, wanting to just die and disappear. It had stormed, and there was a lot of snow. The last thing I remember is running toward a light at the end of the road.

I woke up in a hospital bed the following morning with a priest hovering over me. He had a large cross around his neck and was blessing me. No one who knew me knew I was missing, and the hospital staff began asking me questions. Amidst their questioning, I blacked out again.

That night, I was woken by my parents. When they'd found out that I was missing from the mission president's home, they had driven up from Virginia, which took all day.

The hospital staff explained that a police officer had found me passed out on a bench on a freezing winter morning in only a T-shirt and jeans. They had rushed me to the hospital, unconscious, where they pumped my stomach full of charcoal in an effort to save my life in case I had drugs in my system.

I was depressed that I had to continue living. I also had an overwhelming feeling that life continues after death, and that knowledge depressed me more because it meant that I couldn't simply end.

It was decided that I should be honorably released from my mission and sent home. Once again, I felt like a failure.

Abuse

Every missionary has to give a report of their mission to a local church council after they return home. It is a chance to review what you did during that time. I remember feeling nervous about mine because of the nature of both my returns, but the group of men who made up the council treated me well and congratulated me on my efforts and accomplishments.

As I walked out the door, one of the council members told me he had a job for me and to contact him the following week. I followed up, and after an interview, I was offered a paid real estate internship.

Life seemed to be progressing nicely. I quickly rented a basement apartment by a lake in Reston, and I had the privilege of teaching the gospel to two of my good friends and introducing a third to the missionaries. Those experiences gave me confidence that I could still serve the Lord in a small way after returning home early from my mission. Past that, I was getting a lot of interest and calls from girls I had known in high school, and I took the opportunity to see where it would go with several. I also met a lot of new people through work, and I liked learning about the real estate market.

Meanwhile, over the course of two months at work, my boss—the member of the local church council—continually called me into his office to talk about his addiction to porn. He would ask me to help him stay away from it. Discussing adult magazines in an office setting with an older man always made me very uncomfortable, especially when that man was a member of my church and had a big leadership role in the area.

He also always wanted to exercise at lunch. There was a locker room in the building, and he seemed to enjoy being around men who were in their towels or less. I always wore my towel, and he would tease me for not being man enough to walk nude.

He had done this before with a few returned missionaries and would tell me stories about how they had helped him with his addiction. He was very manipulative and would bring adult magazines into the office and then call me in, trying to get me to look at them. I always refused, and he would say, "Thanks, I need that strength."

One day, he asked me for a ride home because his car was in the shop. As we were driving home, he pulled out a briefcase with several adult magazines. One of them was of men. I asked him to put them away. The look on his face is one I will never forget: He whimpered like a baby and pouted because I wouldn't look or get excited about them. As we pulled up to his house, his wife and kids came out the door to greet him. I felt sick.

His manipulation escalated and came to its peak during a weeklong business trip. He had to go look at properties in New York City and invited me to join him, describing how lucky I was to be traveling as an intern. He booked the Grand Marquis Marriott in Times Square, and when we arrived at the hotel and checked in, he said they had run out of rooms and I would have to share one with him. He even had the audacity to find magazines nearby. While I felt overwhelmed by the situation, he was acting like a young teenager and was very happy.

As we picked our sides of the room and were getting ready for bed, he asked if he could turn a porn show on on the television. I said no. At that time, his wife called. I felt relieved, but he switched personalities on the phone and complained to his wife that he wasn't having a good day. He was trying to make me feel guilty for telling him he couldn't do what he wanted.

After hanging up on the phone, he jumped onto his bed and continued to complain, so I gave in and said, "You do what you want. I'm going to bed."

He turned on the porn and kept asking me to watch, eventually pulling his pants down and playing with himself. From that point on, my world went dark and all my memories are vague. I only remember him offering to massage me, trying to rub my legs, and wanting me to join. I didn't and told him to leave me alone. I went to sleep and woke up the next day traumatized. All I wanted to do was get home.

As soon as I did, I called church authorities and the company's human resources department. I told HR that I didn't want to return to work and explained what had happened. My boss's boss was also a church member, and that man's boss was the president of the company, as well as being a member of the Church of Jesus Christ of Latter-day Saints and my Sunday school teacher. I knew my story wouldn't go over well and I would be heavily questioned.

The man was called in to speak with church authorities. He denied it all, and we had to go back and forth several times before any action was taken. I heard that he was eventually let go by the company.

I just wanted to get away from it all. Even though I'd enrolled at George Mason University, I dropped out and re-enrolled at Ricks College in Idaho, canceling my apartment and driving across the nation to leave Virginia in the past.

Black Clouds Over White Castles

When I arrived at Ricks College for the second time, I was more prepared to be there. Life as a missionary had taught me better study habits, and I was more willing to obey the school's strict rules.

One particular day before school started, I went tubing with some of the football players. On the way home, we got behind a car full of girls. One of the football players knew two girls in the car and tried getting their attention. It did not work, so we decided to follow them to see where they were going. They ended up driving to their apartment, and the football player who knew two of the girls got us invited inside.

One of the girls this football player knew was Lisa Lewis. He had actually taken her to prom his senior year of high school. She was tall and strikingly beautiful, and when I walked in and saw her standing in the back of the room, she grabbed all my attention. We were all introduced, and I was able to get Lisa's number and ask her on a date.

One of my good friends on the football team joined me on that date along with one of Lisa's friends. We went to Pizza Hut and then back to our apartment to watch a movie. Afterward, Lisa distanced herself from me. She had a crush on someone else and wanted to see where it went. Of course, that made me want her more, but there was nothing I could do. I thought that was the end.

At one of the college's weekly devotionals, James E. Faust, who was a member of the church presidency, spoke. He was also a cousin of my grandma's, so I was excited to be there and listened intently to what he said. He talked about careers and up-and-coming fields that would help us be better providers for our families. In particular, he mentioned social work, IT, and health care. Due to the computer job I had in high school and my personal study of computers and programs, including always having a computer at home, I connected with the suggestion of IT. I made up my mind at that time that I would study computers and figure out a way to make a living in that field. This was just a year or two before the internet became widespread, and only the privileged had personal computers at college.

I continued to go on dates, but no one was that interesting and I decided to just focus on school and work. Then one day, I heard a knock on my door and when I answered it, Lisa was standing there. She asked if she could come in. I was surprised but very glad to see her. We decided to go out again.

When the bishop I had worked out my repentance with in my first year of college heard that I was dating Lisa, he called Lisa's father to divulge all those past sins. Of course, that put a big damper in Lisa's parents' minds as to who their daughter was dating. They put a heavy burden of shame on her, and it soon became very apparent that her family did not like me.

But Lisa and I loved to be together. We were good kids and obeyed curfew and all the college's rules. We clicked.[a]

The two of us had very serious conversations about the situation. I never wanted her to feel that I was on the other side, going against her parents. I wanted her to know that I understood their concern. I even tried to end our relationship a few times, but Lisa insisted that we fight for it, so we continued to date that semester and even into the next.

I had decided to try playing football again. Dalton offered to give me $1,000 if I tried out, and I was in the best shape of my life. The coach agreed to let me try out in the spring even though he was upset with me walking off the team my freshman year. I played with the team through spring camp, but it was very apparent that my arm was still damaged from my senior year in high school. At the end of the spring season, I felt that

---

a. Lisa: I didn't really have many boyfriends. I was friends with a lot of guys and hung out with a lot of guys, but I didn't date many guys. When I met Sabe, he was really different. For one thing, he was disciplined because he was trying to play football at the college. He was working out a lot. He was eating really healthy. I was impressed by all of that.

There weren't any red flags at all. Contrary to the rest of my family, I liked that he had a lot more life experience than me and that he had gone through more. It seemed like he had come out as a stronger, more dynamic person. My family members typically steer away from people like that. But I was drawn to it. I didn't want someone boring and sure as heck did not end up marrying someone who was boring.

football needed to be buried for good.

One good thing came from it, though: I took the $1,000 and some other cash I had and bought a ring.

That spring, the drama with Lisa's family was at what seemed to be its highest point. They just didn't accept me. Surprisingly, Lisa's grandfather accepted me and what we were doing, and when I went to see him, he told me to be patient, continue to be good to Lisa, and enjoy this time.

One day, Lisa and I were talking about how hard things were and I said, "Let's just do it. Let's get engaged." I grabbed the ring and took her to the highest point of Rexburg, up where her family had lived at the time she was born. When we arrived at the top of the hill, I got down on one knee and asked her to marry me. I placed the ring on her finger, and just like that, we were engaged.[b]

We decided to get married in the summer, but Lisa struggled with getting her parents to agree to that. She would suggest a date, and they would respond with a lot of hesitancy and pushback. They wanted her to come home and see that what she had decided to do was a mistake.

The semester ended, and both of us went home. After a few weeks of Lisa struggling without support for our relationship, I offered to fly her to Virginia, where we could have a simple marriage ceremony with those who supported us. She agreed, so I flew to Utah to get her. She left her parents' house with her bags, and we stayed in a hotel that night before jumping on a plane back to Virginia. We slept in separate beds, but that night in the hotel became a very sticky point with her family in the weeks to follow.

Eventually, after Lisa's parents saw how serious we were about getting married, they agreed on a date and asked Lisa to return home. She did, and we planned for a quick and small wedding in the Bountiful Utah Temple that summer.

---

b. Lisa: I honestly think that all of the judgment and harassment that my parents were giving me probably got in the way of Sabe and me being able to focus on our relationship with each other. Instead, their animosity was the focus. That was always what we were talking about. We couldn't just be into each other. It was more like, "We need to get married, and we need to get married now because my parents are against us."

In our church culture, you don't have the option of dating someone for very long because there's so much pressure to marry someone soon after you meet them. I feel like if we had dated longer and if I'd continued to push my parents' judgment out of the way, maybe I would have seen for myself that it wasn't the best situation. But then again, maybe not. I was pretty stubborn because I did feel good about marrying him.

Even with all that was going on, our wedding day was a success and a high point in my life. However, as we walked outside of the Bountiful Temple following the ceremony, there was a very dark cloud hanging right over the building throughout the time that we were taking pictures. It seemed to be the only dark and dreary cloud in the sky. Looking back, perhaps it was an omen.[c]

After the wedding, we drove to Park City for our honeymoon, then returned to Virginia, where we rented the same place I had stayed in the summer before.[d] We quickly found work; Lisa was able to land a job working as a receptionist for a global software company making $22,000 a year and I found a job doing support for a software company. I was responsible for answering the phone and helping people with technical issues, which mainly meant troubleshooting bugs and helping people with their passwords. I earned $21,000 a year, and it always bugged me that Lisa was making more. I didn't mind the job, but I enrolled in an IT college for working professionals and was eager to graduate and earn more.

Lisa became pregnant during our first year of marriage. I was impressed that she was able to so easily go to work while dealing with pregnancy, but I also felt guilty about it. She worked full time but didn't want to keep that up after the baby was born, and as her pregnancy progressed, I felt more and more pressure to find a job that could support us without her working.

I learned that Rich, a former colleague of mine who was now an IT department manager at HSO, needed help with IT support for 150 consultants. It was a great opportunity with a lot of growth potential, so I resigned from my job and joined HSO. In the change, I almost doubled my salary.

We had our first child in the Reston Hospital and called her Harper Leslie. Work was coming easily to me, and in our second year of marriage, I got a raise and was able to travel to Holland for work. I loved my job,

---

c. Lisa: I met Sabe shortly after he had that experience with the high counselor, and he was pretty open with me with what had just happened. It was a shocking story and it was a shocking situation, but I didn't really think that it would impact him. No one in my family had any mental illnesses, so I definitely was very, very, very naïve when I married Sabe. I had no idea what I was getting myself into. Now, if my kid was dating someone with bipolar disorder, I'd tell them to run as fast as they possibly could. But I think I'm old enough to know that if I ran away from that, I'd probably be running to another big struggle.

d. Lisa: I think I was relieved to get away.

and Lisa seemed to be happy that she was a full-time mom. We sold my Ford Escort and purchased a brand new 4-Runner. We were very excited to be parents. Life seemed to be going well for us, but the stress of being a father, a full-time student at night, and a full-time employee in the day was mounting. I would work eight hours a day and go to college every night for three to four hours. Sleeping started to be a struggle for me. I would play Age of Empires on the computer until 2 or 3:00 in the morning, when I would eventually fall asleep.

I started to have bouts of depression, and my migraines continued. To cope, I took breaks in my car and isolated myself in my office. At night, my mind seemed to race and come alive. We had dial-up internet, and I would find myself playing Age of Empires and talking with people in AOL chat forums while my wife and baby slept.[e]

Even though I seemed to get little sleep and my energy was inconsistent, I continued to excel at school and work. I was fortunate to learn new technologies at the full height of the dot-com boom. I was eventually promoted to IT manager.

Lisa became a photographer to help supplement our income and to have a profession. I was making $50,000 at my job, and with the additional income, were able to afford to rent and eventually buy a townhouse in Ashburn, Virginia.

As time went on, I started slipping into looking at pornographic images and chatting all night on AOL. I began to have two very different lives, using the computer to disappear into a different reality each night. Looking back, I was losing my moral compass and starting to unravel personally.

Meanwhile, my father, still staying sober, had quit his job but was having success with brokering real estate. He owned and kept horses from Utah on farms all over the country with the idea of breeding them and selling the colts. In reality, he more or less collected horses and owned up to 180. In the process of that, though, he got to know the farmers who were housing his horses, and when they were interested in selling or developing a portion of their farms, Dad was the first to know. He brokered well over $100 million in land deals over the course of a decade.

With Dad sober and making good money, Mom was getting a break

---

e. Lisa: I spent so many years being so livid, so angry at night because he was not sleeping for days and days. I was like, "Dude! You have to sleep. You *have* to sleep."

from the grips of alcoholism that had plagued our family in the early years. She was climbing the ranks at various organizations, and the family seemed to be thriving. All the boys were getting married, finishing up missions, or attending school.[f]

I was only twenty credits shy of completing my college education with an information systems degree when I was offered a job working for a company headquartered in Salt Lake City with my brother Dalton. The offer was too good to not accept, and I made the choice to drop out midway through the semester.

When Lisa was pregnant with Shawn, I approached her and asked if she would want to move to Utah and be close to her family. The company I worked for had me working for a few dot-com startups as a consultant, traveling all over the U.S. installing and configuring various software packages, and I figured I would be able to check in easier and get to know more people if we lived near the company's headquarters. Within three days of asking her, we had packed up our townhome and were on our way to Heber, Utah, where we had found a home to rent near Lisa's parents. The U-Haul we rented would only go 45 miles per hour when climbing some hills, and it constantly blew blue smoke out of the exhaust.

Not long after the move to Utah, the company landed a big deal in Austin, Texas, where a NASA engineer needed an e-commerce website for his patents. I was appointed as the project manager and began traveling to Austin for five days every week.

My habits from high school began to take hold again. I would go to bars by myself and drink, stay awake most of the night and goof off on the internet, and seek drugs, meeting people at bars in Austin and other places to get my hands on marijuana.

My nights and days started to blur. The job was growing so rapidly that I could barely keep up, and I self-medicated to keep pace, doing uppers during the day and downers at night. My intimacy with Lisa took on a different form, with images from the Internet and my former boss's abuse playing out in my head. Those flashing images led me to sink deeper into

---

f. Lisa: After we got married, Chris was sober for a few years. Harper especially got some really good years with him as a grandpa. He spent a lot of time helping her draw or paint or be with the horses. He was always so great with the kids. But as time went on and he started struggling, we didn't want to be around him quite as much. As for Sabe's mom, she was an amazing grandma. She never overstepped her boundaries. She was always really, really respectful of that, and I had a ton of respect for her.

depression and self-medication, and I had a hard time whenever I was home because I didn't have anything to self-medicate with. I felt guilty and ashamed, and I really began to hate the Church of Jesus Christ of Latter-day Saints and Heavenly Father. I blamed Him for the situation.

Soon, I convinced Lisa to move to Austin. I wanted her to be closer so I didn't have to fly home every weekend. By this time, Shawn had been born, yet I couldn't have felt any more disconnected from reality.[g]

We moved into a three-story condo overlooking the Colorado River. Work was going well, and I was making a six-figure salary with bonus in the height of the dot-com boom. We were looking for a home to buy, but I started buying expensive cars, upgrading BMWs every six to ten months in a two-year period, and those purchases increased my debt-to-income ratio, making it harder to qualify for the homes we really wanted.

Dalton purchased a home in Austin, and after a year, both he and I decided to pull the trigger and move to San Antonio. Lisa and I found a home in the outskirts, and Dalton moved closer to the city.

Some time after moving to San Antonio, Dalton and I both joined a different company. This one was headquartered in Lehi, Utah, which meant we had to travel to Utah regularly again.

---

g. Lisa: Sabe doesn't remember a lot of our life. Like, Shawn as a baby. He doesn't remember that, which is super sad.

The Dark Web

While my financial life was excelling, my personal life, which was hidden from Lisa and the kids, was a disaster. My job sent me to various places around the nation and eventually to Central and South America, and when I traveled, I spent my nights drinking in bars and looking for weed. I was taking ephedrine pills regularly so I could keep up the high energy I needed for work, and the ephedrine made me explosive, volatile, and extremely moody. I couldn't sleep, and when I was home, I would spend hours driving around downtown San Antonio. When I was on the road, I would be up all night on the computer playing games, chatting with random people, or looking at pornography. I only got a few hours of sleep each night.

I quickly got bored with alcohol, weed, and ephedrine and started seeking ecstasy/MDMA on the internet. I would buy as much as I could at once so I didn't have to meet up with dealers that often.

One night, I met with a drug dealer in a quiet neighborhood and bought two hundred hits of acid. Afterward, I told Lisa I would be out of town and instead got a hotel just ten miles away. That was a bad idea. I had no idea how to do acid, and I was by myself.

When I got situated in the hotel, I pulled out the sheets of acid, put a tab on my tongue, and waited a few minutes. Nothing happened, so I put another one on my tongue.

Five to ten minutes passed, and still nothing.

So I took another.

I must have applied a total of four or five within a twenty-minute period when all of sudden, the acid hit—bad. I had only been in the hotel for about an hour when I started to hallucinate. The worst was when I made the mistake of looking in the mirror. What I saw there was evil and horrific.

After I tore myself away from the mirror, I got paranoid and thought I was going to get caught with the drugs. Flushing the sheets of acid down the toilet, I left. I had a pipe for weed with me, and I hid that in a trash can just outside the elevator door.

As I hurried out of the hotel, I saw a country band's bus and police escort in the parking lot. Thinking that there might have been cameras in the hallway and they had recorded me, I rushed back up to the hotel room. I was hallucinating and hearing things, and I felt very scared. I decided to call Lisa.

That was the first time I admitted to her that I was doing drugs and I needed help. Of course, she was upset that I had lied about being out of town when I was just down the road, doing drugs in a hotel room. Even still, I begged her to help me. I needed her to be on the phone with me while I attempted to drive home. She took pity on me, and finally, I got the nerve to go down to the car again and drive home. Lisa stayed on the phone the entire time.

When I got home, I tried calming down, but I couldn't. Instead, I spent hours pacing the floor, talking to Lisa to keep from thinking about the things I had seen in the mirror. I tried lying down a few times, but whenever I closed my eyes, I saw images that freaked me out. I literally felt like I was being dragged down to hell and death. One delusion was of being in a dark and dingy basement. There were chains hanging from the ceiling and only a single window. Every time I got closer to the window, I would see Satan trying to come in through it.

I paced all night and into the morning, walking back and forth until I was absolutely exhausted and the effects of the acid wore off. The next day was terrible. The sun came up and I had to face the day—and my family—with no sleep. Even though the acid had mostly left my system, I felt schizophrenic and continued to see shadows in the corners of my eyes. Every bright light or sound was amplified. I tried to hide my severe depression and suicidal thoughts from my kids and co-workers, but that night, something had changed for my family and me. The reality of our lives, the drug abuse and lying, was now visible.

I had massive bouts of anxiety and depression, and my thoughts would race. Ecstasy would calm me down and make the pain go away, so I stocked up on it for my work trips to Brazil and Mexico, using it to relax on the airplane and to get through the nights. After those sleepless nights, I would drink energy drinks until my meetings were over and I could take more ecstasy. My routine on business trips was to have a meeting for an hour and then crash, doing drugs in the hotel. I would be high for days, sometimes taking up to sixteen pills a week to maintain the high. Coming off those binges was very hard; I would plummet into a depression and think about committing suicide.[h]

Ecstasy was too harsh, and I couldn't control my days because my energy and mood swings were inconsistent, so I decided to plunge into the world of cocaine. One night at home while talking on the internet, I found a dealer who would sell an ounce to me for $2,000. He lived in Corpus Christi, which was about two hours away. I agreed to make the trek the next day.

He wanted to meet me in a public place so the deal wouldn't be

---

h. Lisa: When Harper was in preschool, it was a really, really bad time. Sabe was always more manic, but at that time, he was a lot more depressed. One night in bed, he was like, "Lisa, I don't have a single good memory of anything."

I said, "We have two young kids. There's so much to look forward to."

But he literally had no hope at all. Finally, I was just like, "Do you even want us around?"

He couldn't answer.

That was devastating. Afterward, I actually called my dad, who was in Utah. It was the middle of the night. I said, "Dad, will you come and get us?"

It was kind of like he had been waiting for that phone call. He just said, "I'll get in a moving truck right now and come get you."

Harper was four, and when I told her we were leaving, her thoughts were, "No, no. I don't want to leave. What are we going to do with my kittycats?" That kind of thing.

But before long, I realized that Sabe was mentally ill and it wasn't fair of me to ask him questions like that. He wasn't well enough to give a proper response. He wasn't doing this on purpose. He wasn't trying to hurt us. If he was so sick, how could I leave?

So I called my dad back a few hours later and essentially said, "Actually, never mind. I'm going to stay in this very abusive situation." I had to explain to everybody: If Sabe had cancer, would I leave him? Absolutely not. The tricky thing with a mental illness is it affects your brain, so it affects your emotions and it affects everything. It affects your personality and the decisions you make. You can't always just leave someone. I felt like there was way more good inside of him than bad. He deserved a happy life more than anybody.

I definitely didn't think that it was okay, though. It wasn't a good situation to be in. I just realized that at that moment in time, he really was not doing well, so I couldn't just leave. It was always a very, very fine balance between believing that this was a mental illness and feeling bad about it but also believing I was in a really, really bad situation.

detected by police. Buying drugs off the internet was not as policed in the late '90s as it is today, but there were still a lot of risks. He gave me detailed instructions so that we wouldn't see each other during the transaction. The trade was going to happen in a bar, and the cocaine would be in a light fixture in the bathroom. I was supposed to exchange the cocaine for $2,000 cash.

I drove to Corpus from San Antonio the next night, and when I arrived, I was very nervous about going into a half-empty bar and performing the deal. I went straight back to the bathroom, found the bag of coke, and left the cash. Walking out of the bathroom was surreal.

As I walked back out to my car, a guy came up to me in the parking lot and said, "Hey dude, I'm glad you aren't a cop." We became friends and decided to get a hotel room to party that night.

It was my first time doing coke. The drug gave me the feeling I was looking for, and now I had a good contact.

I was inconsistent with my work ethic, and as the dot-com crash approached, my career and personal choices started to catch up with me. I was binging and pulling all-nighters either on the road or, by lying to my wife, in a local bar and hotel. My focus was always on finding my next fix.

I would score drugs and bring them home, then hide in the guest room and get on AOL Chat or look at adult content on the internet. When I finally fell asleep and woke up the next day, I would feel depressed and lie in a dark room all day, wanting to be left alone.[i][j]

I spent time in depression and bipolar chat rooms and made friends online. I was always amazed at the nightlife on the internet and the crazy conversations people would have. Everyone seemed to be role-playing their deep secrets and desires. Later in life, I realized they were really role-playing the abuse they had endured and couldn't let go of. Darkness fed on darkness, and people seemed to be stuck in their past as it twisted and became a tool for them to justify their current behavior. I was in the same predicament.[k]

---

i. Lisa: He was so not present. He was not feeling any of the emotions that he should have been feeling. It was really hard to be okay with that.

j. Lisa: When we were in San Antonio, I was like this mama squirrel with her two little babies: I didn't care what else was going on with the world, I was just keeping them safe and close.

k. Lisa: The times we were living in San Antonio when he wasn't sleeping and he was in those chat rooms all night long with the door locked—it was so unnerving.

One night, I met a girl who said she used to be a cheerleader in high school and while visiting New York City, a man attacked her sexually in a Marriott Marquis hotel elevator in Times Square. I was shocked because that was the same hotel where I had been preyed upon by the church leader while on a business trip. I told her my story, and we immediately had a connection.

We began talking every night. The girl finally sent me a picture of herself, and we seemed to be very interested in each other. She was a BYU student in Utah, and since I was traveling to Utah often, I suggested a few times that we should meet up. She always seemed to have a reason why she couldn't.

Soon, I booked a hotel in Utah for a week, mainly so I could talk on the phone with this particular girl. I was thinking about leaving my wife, having delusions of how my life should be. I ran out of drugs while in the hotel, I couldn't sleep, and I seemed to be fixed on Jesus that week. I spent a few nights drawing graphs and timelines from recent history and the Bible and overlaying them on the wall to pinpoint when He would come. I was obsessed with it. I remember finally coming to the conclusion that Jesus would come on a Thursday at 3:30 p.m.

Whenever I talked with the girl, I would try very hard to convince her to meet with me. She finally agreed to meet at a BYU parking lot, so I got in my rental and drove to the parking lot, then waited in the car. No one came, and she wouldn't answer her phone. I felt very uneasy.

All of sudden, a girl came up to my car. I rolled down the window. It wasn't the girl in the picture, but she introduced herself as a friend of the girl and told me her friend couldn't go through with the meeting. While she was talking, I noticed another girl looking at us from a bench. I shouted her name, and she stood up and came over. It was the girl I had felt a strong connection with. She was crying, and I felt sick. The girl who stood in front of me was quite large and looked nothing like the girl in the picture she had sent me. She later told me she had gained a bunch of weight after she was attacked. To this date, I don't know if her story is true or not. I just hugged her and left.

Talking to her there in the parking lot, I had a moment of clarity. I started to realize that my marriage and life would probably come to an end. I was guilty. A fool. A sick man.

My soul felt heavy. I finally realized something must be wrong with me, and I finally wanted to get help.

Excommunication

I started reading about bipolar disorder because I knew it was in my genes and I regularly experienced some of the extreme behavior I had often heard associated with mania. Along with reading, I started talking with people in AOL bipolar chat rooms. I would stay up many nights and be amazed at manic people's level of creativity and energy as their words appeared on my screen. I could sense the worlds their minds expounded on and painted. We chatted about the most random ideas. Many of them were sober but manic, and many others were manic and using drugs.

I wanted to act out in retaliation, but I knew that behavior wouldn't be received with open arms. In the end, I decided that turning myself in was the best thing I could do to save my family and somehow get help.

So when I came home from Utah, I turned myself in to my wife.[1] Then, knowing I was facing excommunication, I suggested that I turn myself in to the church.

I was mad at my mom and dad for how we grew up and for how hard my mom was on me.

It was hard not to be mad at God for the things that had happened to me after serving a mission.

I was mad at my college bishop and at Lisa's parents for judging me and not giving me a chance.

---

1. Lisa: I was definitely in shock through a lot of this. I was thinking, "I cannot believe this is my life." But at the same time, my older sister was going through infertility and finding out that she would never be able to have kids, and I actually remember thinking, "I wouldn't want to trade positions with her."

I hated the men who had hurt me, and I was very angry with the church.

But I still knew I was in the wrong.

I scheduled time to talk with the stake president[1] of our local area.[m] My sins were many and very egregious, and I was very open and honest about them while talking to him. I told him about my porn addiction, infidelity in my marriage, drug abuse, and poor decisions. I didn't hold anything back. I wanted to come clean, and I truly needed help. I also explained that because I had been abused, I had a hard time with male church leaders and that the abuse and judgment I received from leaders and members of the church had made me feel betrayed. I told the stake president that my attitude toward Heavenly Father was bitter. Finally, at the end, I told him I might be bipolar.

That's when I learned he was judgmental and abusive, not the type of person to seek help and repentance through. He said he didn't believe in bipolar disorder, and one of his first questions was whether my wife and I had graduated from high school. My takeaway from the meeting was that he thought I was uneducated white trash.

Lisa and I decided that we needed a new start. Dad had just finished brokering a 2,000-acre estate just outside of Waterford, Virginia, and had been hired by the estate to run its farm and horse operation. In exchange for

---

1. In the Church of Jesus Christ of Latter-day Saints, a stake president leads multiple wards (congregations) within a specific geographical area.

m. **Lisa:** I knew there wasn't anything that I could do to hurt or to help Sabe, but I also knew this wasn't just going to go away on its own. I looked at the situation very medically. It was hard for me to look at it in any other light. I didn't think anything that I could do would help, and for a long time, I didn't even think that praying would make a difference. I didn't think prayer would take that diagnosis away or make things better. I didn't think anything could fix it. So I lost a lot of faith. I lost a lot of hope.

The biggest turning point for me was when we were sitting down with our stake president and he said, "I truly believe that the Spirit has power to heal." For some reason, that gave me a lot of hope. And I think it probably gave Sabe a lot of hope. At that point, he had to believe that he could get on the right track, and I think the stake president got him to think, "I've spent all these years making bad decisions, and maybe, just maybe, if I could start making good decisions, I could actually get some help."

After that, it felt like the times in between the relapses became less frequent. But you know, there were still times when it would happen or he wouldn't come home and he would disappear and it was always at the wrong time, whether it was a holiday or someone's birthday. It was such a rollercoaster of bipolar, where there were always good moments but the bad moments were just devastating.

helping put the deal together, Dad was able to buy the lower part of the 2,000 acres at a discount. There was a late 1800s home and barn on those acres; Dalton purchased over fifty acres to help secure the property, and Mom and Dad had the other fifty acres with the home and barn. Sight unseen, Lisa and I expressed interest in living in the home. We enjoyed projects and fell in love with the idea of living in an old home on horse property.

My boss agreed to move us from San Antonio back to Virginia. To please my family and through a half-hearted interest in getting better, I started seeking mental health doctors who could diagnose my problem and prescribe whatever was needed to help me sleep and deal with all the anxiety I felt. Before we packed up and left, I visited with the church-sponsored AA and started seeing doctors about my depression. One of the first therapists I saw was recommended by my bishop. That was my introduction to talk therapy and the beginning of me opening up about my past and current problems.

After moving to Virginia, I received a letter of excommunication from the church in the mail, revoking my membership and suspending my baptism and the ordinances I went through in the temple. They didn't have a disciplinary court for me, which is policy. I felt hurt and very judged by the stake president, but by then I was used to disrespect from some leaders in the church. Besides that, church leaders were not the reason I turned myself in and sought help.

I was okay with being excommunicated because I knew I needed help. I was willing to pay the price, whatever that meant. Later, I learned that excommunication is part of the process the church uses to help bring someone back into good standing and it shouldn't be looked at as a negative action.

Chris and the bishop at the time, Bishop Kevin Ryker, became friendly. Chris had painted a couple of large pictures for him, and Bishop Ryker paid him $2,000.

In June 1998, Ethan and Ami were married in the Logan Utah Temple, and we held a wedding ceremony for them at Selma, a beautiful plantation estate built in the early 1800s [in Leesburg, Virginia]. Chris had negotiated the sale of it, and at this reception, Bishop Ryker asked Chris to help him find a similar property for him to invest in. So the next phase of our life began. It took us from the city to the country and on another roller coaster ride because the drinking began shortly thereafter.

Chris did find a fabulous property for Bishop Ryker to invest in. It was a 2,000-acre estate.[1] There was another interested partner who wanted to invest as well, so a partnership was formed between Ryker and David Talton with Chris being a beneficiary by being able to work for the partnership in running the business on the property and [purchasing] 100 acres of the 2,000. This opportunity had a lot of promise because Chris would have a regular income with the potential to earn bonuses and even develop some of his own business.

It was almost too good to be true, and it was short-lived. The partnership soured, and Chris was pushed out of the opportunities altogether. However, he was able to purchase the 100 acres and that is what we salvaged from that experience.

This was a very difficult time for me because I was the leader of the women's group in the church and Bishop Ryker was the head of the entire congregation. The two of us had to work very closely in the organization. What I had hoped was going to be a good, positive experience for Chris with the church turned out to be the opposite and at this time, he quit going to church and planned to move from the city to the country. This made my relationship with Bishop Ryker very awkward.

I will never forget the horror Lisa had on her face when we first saw the old house we would be living in.[n] She broke down in tears, and when we walked in the door and saw all the work that needed to be done, it just got worse. Everything on the outside and inside had to be redone, and it would take several years and tens of thousands of dollars to make it work

---

1. There was a farm and horses on the land when they purchased it.

n. Lisa: The idea sounded great until we actually agreed to move. One of my first times there was to scope out the work that needed to be done, and when I saw it, I wanted to run away. Everywhere I looked, it was just so much work. Water, the furnace, the toilet, the uneven things, the heater, the lights ... everything. It was a lot. You don't always want to bring two young kids into that scenario, and you also have to know that I had never lived in a rural area like that.

to her liking. Our San Antonio home had been a very well built single family home in a busy neighborhood with all modern amenities, and in contrast, old heart pine wood floors were this home's only saving grace. They were original and seemed to have been sanded and recoated in recent years. I loved all the old marks, the wear and tear. In some ways, I thought the house represented me.

Despite my efforts at seeing a therapist and attending the church-sponsored twelve-step addiction recovery program, I started reconnecting with friends from high school, hanging out in bars until late into the night, and buying ecstasy and cocaine. My coke use escalated, and I was spending thousands of dollars a month trying to find reasons to be out of town so I could have space to party. Every attempt to be clean and sober was overshadowed with opportunities to get in trouble. I always wanted to self medicate to change the emotions and anxiety I felt. To this day, I am the same way; when your moods are all over the place and your chemistry is depressed or manic, you seek to change it with whatever you can get your hands on. A quick fix was always around the corner and easily justified. Without medicine to balance or limit the mania, it's nearly impossible to live a normal life or to dampen the impulsivity, compulsion and shifts in moods.

At that time, none of the medications I tried helped with sleep or anxiety. How could they when my heart was only halfway in and I enjoyed getting high?

It was very hard to buy coke while living out in the country, so chasing drugs became my life.º It was a very dark time. I would spend sleepless nights in an apartment we had refurbished in the barn, checking the windows every fifteen minutes to see if anyone was coming down to interrupt me.

On one particular day while I was on a coke binge, I went to a Porsche dealership and purchased a convertible Porsche 968 without even test driving it. I saw it on the lot, walked into the showroom, and bought it. That meant I had two sports cars. I then proceeded to binge for a few days, avoiding home and lying to my family, saying that I was on a business trip.

---

o. Lisa: I never actually saw any of Sabe's cocaine or anything, but I did find a lot of pens with the ink tube taken out of them because that's what he'd use to snort it. I would find them in his car, and I could see the residue on them.

The company I was working for was not meeting its goals, which resulted in an executive turnover and me being laid off for the first time in my life. I was paying $2,500 in monthly car payments and $2,000 in rent, we weren't quite finished with the house renovations,[p] and I had a very expensive drug problem and no job. Over the course of several months, all our money was gone and my cars were taken by the banks.[q] I will never forget the feeling of failure I had while watching our Land Rover being lifted on a flatbed tow truck. I had disappointed my wife. The Porsche was taken next, but that was less stressful because Lisa thought we should never have had it in the first place. We lived on a dirt road, and a convertible two-door Porsche was a luxury item and an added expense.

I was able to secure an old car for us, but the tires were bald and we couldn't afford to replace them. To pay our rent, we took over cleaning the barn and the horse stalls that were rented out. I picked up a job selling custom closets at night and was paid under the table on commissions only.

Lisa and I eventually met and were hired by a neighbor down the road who sold mozzarella cheese at Whole Foods and at farmers markets on the weekend. I would drive to Maryland to collect the milk early every morning, then help to process it. I would deliver the cheese to Whole Foods after making it on the weekdays, and on the weekends, Lisa and I would sell the cheese at two different markets.

Those three jobs gave us enough to get by,[r] and Lisa also took odd jobs painting walls, cleaning homes, and doing whatever else she could find. We didn't have health care, though, so I picked up a fourth part-time job selling used cars. That company provided me with a second car, which

---

p. Lisa: When Sabe lost his job, all of the work that we were doing on the house came to a screeching halt.

q. Lisa: Sabe losing his job was pretty scary. I remember thinking, "Just as long as he finds something within a month, maybe two at the most ..." "As long as we don't have to start living on credit cards ..." But he didn't find a job right away and we were getting more and more in debt. That made me realize how sick he was.

r. Lisa: This situation started going on for so long, and with our two kids being so young, it got to the point of focusing on survival pretty quick. I felt like every bad thing that could happen was happening to us at that point, and I couldn't believe it. I didn't give up, but I was losing hope that things were going to change. We were just always going to be in this survival mode.

But as devastating as our finances were, it was also somewhat empowering to see how Sabe and I were working together. I think that was the first time that we had to really work hard together to make ends meet.

was a great perk, but the car allowance and health care zeroed out my paycheck.

If I did anything during that time that was positive, it would be that I tried to provide money for my wife and two small children. However, I couldn't kick my drug problem, and my bipolar episodes were spinning out of control. I made many poor decisions. On one particular night, Lisa came home after cleaning toilets and opened our credit statement to find that I had taken several cash advances to support my bad habits.[s]

I wasn't connected, and I'm sure it crushed Lisa every day to be around me. If I ever showed moments of clarity, moments that gave hope, they were short-lived.[t]

---

s. Lisa: In the midst of all of this, I was getting the credit card bills and seeing cash advances for $300, $400, $500, or $600, and I knew all of those cash advances were for cocaine. It was just kind of like, "What is the point of us working our butts off if you're just gonna blow this kind of money?" I definitely exploded a lot of times, and I gave a lot of ultimatums. But when he was doing drugs so often, I couldn't even get through to him, and he probably forgot about it. It was kind of like him yelling at Chris when Chris wasn't sober. It was so pointless. But I just kept screaming at him.

t. Lisa: I had to have a lot of faith that because this is medical, it can be cured. It's not always a death sentence.

Rebaptism and Relapse

I did not want to move, but Chris had done his best to support the family for twenty years living in the suburbs and he was itching to get back to country life. I was determined that I would create some boundaries. I would contribute to the family living, but I would not contribute toward any of the investment and making the business run. I was very clear with Chris about this. I could see that I could be stretched beyond my capacity very easily.

However, I felt it was my turn to be supportive of his goals and objectives. To complicate matters, ... I lost my job with Franklin Covey in August 2001, but in a way, I thought perhaps that was a sign that it was Chris's turn to take the lead. It was very chaotic, looking back.

We had let our son Sabe and his family move into the little farmhouse on the 100 acres, so we did not really have any place to move. We had sold fifty of the acres to an acquaintance in order to help finance the other fifty. Chris wanted to build a horse barn and build an apartment on top of it and then eventually build a home on the property, so we had an architectural drawing drafted while we were in the process of selling our home. We put our townhouse on the market on September 11, 2001. I remember the day very well!

The townhouse did not sell for months, and I wondered if that was a sign that we should just stay where we were. The previous year, we had taken Alec out of the Reston schools in anticipation of our move and put him in the Loudoun system. We felt justified in this because we owned property there. However, Alec was expelled because he was not sleeping in a home in Loudoun County. This was humiliating for Alec and, of course, for us. Even though we felt compelled to fight it, we were informed that if we did and we lost, we would be charged for the tuition for the time that Alec had already spent there, which was over $10,000. So we moved him back to Reston until the actual move.

Finally, on December 17, we got a contract on the townhouse and planned to move out by January 15. Alec felt his world was crashing around him. He had lived in Reston his whole life (sixteen years), he had friends on every corner, he was well-liked, and he was a very well-adjusted young man. He had already had a bad experience in Loudoun, and he was not anxious to go back.

Regardless of how Alec and I felt, we sold our home and moved to Loudoun to be supportive of Chris's endeavors. This was a very difficult move because we had nowhere to move to. We stored all our furniture and moved in with our son Sabe and his family. This, of course, was to be temporary ... while we built the barn with the apartment. However, because of zoning, that plan was foiled and there we were with no options. We lived with Sabe and Lisa and family for five months.

To Chris's credit, he was proactive in procuring a little farmhouse that needed some renovation, and we negotiated a deal with the owner to make the improvements in lieu of a 3-year lease. We went about fixing up the little house, and we made it quite comfortable and homey and enjoyed living there until Alec graduated from high school in 2004. During this time, I consulted and had a part-time job with Corporate University Enterprise. I mostly worked from home, and I enjoyed the country life.

The drinking during these years was very sporadic, and I would occasionally find evidence (an empty bottle falling out of the truck). Sabe, however, tells me of many incidences that he witnessed during this time that showed the drinking was creeping back into our lives. Sabe said he would see the truck on the hill at night and know that his father was sitting there drinking. Also, discontent and grandiosity began to increase.

During these years, Chris pursued building a horse business. I was very clear with my boundaries. I was not going to invest in this business. I would help to provide for household expenses, but I was not interested in investing in a horse business. I had a lot of anger and resentment toward Chris during this time. I did not understand him, and we began to drift apart.

In December of 2003, our son Josh was married to Jessica. The marriage was in the Washington DC Temple, and the bishop at the time encouraged Chris to prepare himself to attend the temple and provide priesthood leadership for the family. He asked Chris what he was afraid of, and Chris answered, "I am afraid of who I will see there!" I felt sorry and sad for him. This was the humiliating type of behavior I would get when it came to the church.

Also in terms of business, there were a lot of other roller coaster activities going on. Chris was continuing to broker some land deals, and this was during the time of the real estate boom. He brokered a large deal with a commercial piece of property in Leesburg. This was with Alan Henricks, who at the time was an executive . . . . The 126 acres was purchased by Alan [and another investment group for just over] $6 million. He supposedly gave Chris 3% interest in the property [from his portion]. This property has supposedly grown in value to approximately over $50 million.

Shortly after this deal, Chris speculated on a property to subdivide for residential homes. This speculation required him to contribute $125,000, which he made arrangements for with a private investor for 14% interest! This loan was to be guaranteed with the equity of the little farm in Virginia, which required my notarized signature.

Chris did not discuss this loan with me until he had the

> papers and was ready to sign. I was furious and told him I would not sign such a ridiculous document and he swore and called me a bitch. I eventually signed under duress and told him I did not intend to make any of the payments. This loan went on for years. Sometimes Chris would make the payments, but mostly, he just continued to sign documents with the increased interest tacked on. By the time this note had to be paid a year and a half ago, I had to come up with $180,000 to keep the farm from foreclosure on the second mortgage, which would have left our son and his family homeless. I have continued to make all the payments on the little farm.
>
> This situation was one of the lowest points in my life, and by the time it rolled around, I was yo-yo-ing in and out of the relationship. I would leave for a month or so, each time hoping Chris would find his way back into AA and some sanity would return into our lives. It never worked, and I was becoming more insane in the process.

The housing market was booming, and companies were hiring in droves. A counselor in our local bishopric worked for a large flooring company in the Washington, D.C., area, and he approached me and asked me to come in for an interview. After being laid off for close to two years, it was a blessing. I had high hopes of getting a job and kicking my drug problem to the curb so that I could better provide for my family.

I did well in the interview, and they offered me the job with a salary that was comparable to the peak of my dot-com days. With commissions, I could be back in six figures again. I would have to drive to Manassas, which took about fifty minutes each way, but I was very grateful to have the chance at a stable income and insurance for my family. I felt connected to society again. When I came home and delivered my news, it was a very bright moment.

When I was out of a job, I had given my BMW to a friend, and he took over making payments on it. Now I was able to take it back. I was also able to buy a newer car for the family. Another thing that had happened while I was laid off, and this one was positive, was that I had started teaching myself how to play the guitar. I always loved music and creating but struggled to play sheet music or cover songs, so I began writing my own songs. On one particular day at work, we were all sitting around as a group and I started talking about music with Craig, who was in the estimating department. I told him I was writing songs, and he invited me to his house so he could listen to my demos.

We immediately became good friends. Craig had a basement full of recording gear and instruments from his days of being in a band, and after months of recording and experimenting with different songs, we decided to start a band. One of our customers played drums, and he joined. His name was Phil. Over the course of seven years, we wrote eighty songs and played in bars and mini clubs in the D.C. area.

Music was a key tool in my life for putting my frustrations and experiences down on paper. In an odd way, it gave me something to live for. I was by no means a pro, but writing music gave me more balance and a healthy outlet to express my pain. I wrote about my visions, about memories, or about the painful emotions I felt about particular subjects. One song I wrote was about feeling suicidal one night when I was alone in the house, looking out of a window in our master bedroom. The bedroom was painted red, car lights would periodically pass by on the dirt road in front of the house, and I could feel suicide in my chest as I took breaths. We lived in rolling valleys of forest, miles from the city, and the feeling of desolation was very apparent in my soul. In another song, written when I felt more manic, I sang about my experiences with walls. The first verse was about me trying to kiss my girlfriend when I was six or seven. She ducked while my eyes were closed, and I leaned over and kissed the wall. The second verse was about being pushed into a wall and chipping my tooth. The third verse was in the present, looking at a picture of my family hanging on the wall.

I thought I was pretty creative, and I was narcissistic enough to think I could be a rock star. But to be completely honest, I felt like a dummy when we performed for an audience. My idea of creating music was doing it in a studio. We recorded a few albums in Cue Studio in Falls Church, and I thoroughly enjoyed that. I didn't enjoy playing in bars at all. My music was never written to be in a bar, where most people want to hear covers and happy music. It was more depressive and would bring down the mood of the bar. It was not fun packing around equipment, playing to empty clubs, or singing in front of people I didn't connect with. With my dad's drinking habits, I didn't like being around alcohol, either. That, of course, was a double standard. Every time I played at an open mic, a bar, or mini club, I was high. I would sneak bumps in the bathrooms before going onstage. The only fun I had was being with Craig and Phil, creating noise.

Every time there was progress or good news like this new job, I would try hard to do the right thing for a day or two, but it would wear off quickly. This time around, I didn't want to give up my ability to write and be creative even if doing so would have also meant the end of the terrible swings from drug abuse and bipolar episodes. I found better places to buy drugs, and by this time, I had more money and could buy larger amounts that would last longer. Somehow, I managed to take on more responsibilities and manage teams at work. I must have shown potential, but looking back, my follow-through and consistency struggled. I would go for days without sleep, and having to work without sleep was hell. I would often sneak off and sleep in my car while coming down from the drugs during work. Many times, I felt like a zombie. My depression was severe.

I always tried my hardest to come up with excuses to give Lisa for being out late, which of course frustrated her. Many times, I would disappear all night or sneak into the barn apartment, where I would be up all night in a paranoid frenzy. It was a very dark time in my life; pornography and drugs controlled me every day. I wanted help and to stop, but I couldn't seem to and my medications weren't working due to my lifestyle and choices. I tried to keep attending church and tried to keep up with my job. My family life was struggling.[u]

I continued to seek a psychiatrist and came across a quiet little Jewish lady in Bethesda, Maryland. During my first visit, I described all my problems and struggles and she simply said, "You need sleep. Once you get sleep, we can figure out the next problem." She prescribed a heavy dose of Seroquel, a medicine that is used for schizophrenic and bipolar patients, and sent me home.[v]

---

u. Lisa: I have always found a lot more comfort in my kids than I have in Sabe because I had to keep them so close to me. They were my only source of comfort and peace. It's still kind of like that today.

When the kids asked, I think I probably told them that Dad wasn't doing well. Or I'd say he was down in the barn. Which was where he was most of the time. Harper probably remembers the most from this time.

v. Lisa: I tell people all the time that bipolar is very treatable. But you have to stay treated, you know?

I will never forget my first night of taking that medication. After about twenty minutes, I felt as if my brain was being suffocated or choked to sleep. The Seroquel was shutting off my brain, and it was a very intense feeling. I felt claustrophobic and jumped out of bed to pace the floor. On a normal night, my mind explodes with colors, visions, and unrealistic ideas of what I want to do the next day. Seroquel put a stop to that. About an hour after taking the medicine, I was asleep. During the middle of the night, the medication was so intense that I peed the bed.

Seroquel's effects would last until early afternoon, and getting up and driving an hour to work was a huge struggle. I felt numb, and my brain did not function well. However, I started having longer periods of sobriety, and with the medication, I was able to sleep. I learned that sleep helps me reset my body's chemicals, something I need if I want to be able to function the next day.

She and I were constantly fighting; on one occasion while Lisa was pregnant with Addie,[w] she chased me out of the house, tried to hit me after an argument, and slipped and fell. I ran to her, trying to console my nine-month pregnant wife, and she slapped me away. I felt terrible and disappeared into the barn apartment.

Addie, our third child, was born at the time Harper was due for baptism. I wanted to be better, and I wanted to baptize Harper myself. My father had not been able to baptize me when I was eight because of worthiness issues, and here I faced the same dilemma. In a great gift to me, Harper waited a year for me to baptize her,[x] which gave me something to fight my addictions for. It worked for a time and helped build my confidence that I could be a worthy father, husband, and contributor to society.

We made it to the waters of baptism in 2006.[y] For those who think you

---

w. Lisa: Getting pregnant with Addie gave me a lot of hope. For so long, I didn't think we would have more kids. I thought, "He's already fathered two children and this could be a really bad situation." Then things started to get better, and when I got pregnant, I felt like it was such a blessing. But there were still some really bad times while I was pregnant with her.

x. Lisa: Sabe really wanted to be the one who baptized Harper and blessed Addie. We baptized Harper when she was about nine and blessed Addie when she was about one, one and a half. We did both of them on the same day.

y. Lisa: Sabe was baptized again, and what I didn't realize then was that he was high the night before his baptism. I found out about that later. I'm surprised I didn't know, because I knew all of the signs, for the most part. I was just happy that it was happening.

need to wait until everything is perfect before taking the next step, I advise you to rethink your strategy. We are all wounded, prideful, and imperfect souls, and we all need help along the way.

Over the course of the next few years, I continued to struggle with drug abuse and keeping up with the demands of family and work.[z] A few times a month, I would cross a bridge into Georgetown and pick up an ounce at the gas station on the corner. Coming off the drugs each night and trying to work was nearly impossible, but I somehow managed to do the bare minimum to keep my job. The abuse became so bad, I would find myself in large retail bathroom stalls for hours. At work, I would hide in empty spaces and disappear for similar lengths of time. I struggled to make it home on time and would drive on the backcountry roads of northern Virginia at night, avoiding Lisa's calls.

There were times when I would manipulate Lisa so I could get back into the house. Once after being high all night in the barn, I knew I had to come up with something dramatic to get her to let me in the house so I could sleep and get to work in a few hours, so I took a knife, cut my arm all up, and came into the house bleeding. It seemed to work, and I was able to get to work the next day. Soon after, I remember Lisa telling me she would leave if this kept up.[A]

The building industry was starting to struggle in the late 2000s, and a few months after Lisa gave me that ultimatum, I was laid off.

I was out of money, laid off from work, and about to lose my family.

---

z. Lisa: On Addie's first birthday (this was before Sabe's re-baptism), my brother and his family were staying with us and I had put in a lot of effort for her birthday party. Then Sabe had a relapse and didn't show up. I couldn't believe it. No matter what was happening or how enticing I made it for him to come home, it didn't matter. He was going to fall off the wagon. For me, him missing that party was the lowest point out of everything. I thought things were so much better before that moment, and I had felt like that birthday party was a big milestone—not just in her life, but for us too.

A. Lisa: I gave Sabe a lot of ultimatums. A lot. But then long periods of time would pass before he would relapse. I would get my hopes up, and then they'd all come crashing down. Then I'd get my hopes up again.

I don't know if I ever necessarily drew a really, really hard line. I always just had hope that he actually really cared and that he didn't want this. He wanted the good life. I will say this too: There were a lot of times when I was scared to draw a line because I thought that he could hurt himself. I felt like I had to be really careful with what I said and with what I threatened because he could easily have taken his own life.

In the end, I think I did the right thing in having hope and staying.

That was my turning point. Nothing magical, just in a pathetic spot to be in.[B]

I tried harder to make better decisions in every aspect of my life, including taking medication, spending more time with my kids, attending church more frequently, and fighting the urges of drugs and pornography. It was the hardest to fight these urges when I was left alone; I didn't have a lot of hobbies and positive influences. I eventually found a position as a regional manager for a Fortune 500 company in the building industry. We began doing more as a family. The songs I wrote and performed with the band became more positive. I took baby steps.[C]

Over the course of about eighteen months, I only had two relapses. In one, Lisa was in Utah and I just stayed home and did coke. The other one happened when I was scheduled to be out of town for a business trip and I thought I could get away with it. I drove into a rough area of D.C., met up with an old connection, bought two 8 balls, and made my way to a hotel. I had meetings the next day and just wanted to do enough to enjoy it and then get some sleep. Well, that didn't happen.

Once I got started doing drugs, I couldn't stop until they were gone, and I had a lot that time. I turned off my phone, and over the course of three days and two nights, I sat frozen in a corner of that hotel room and consumed both 8 balls. I was so paranoid about getting caught that I did not leave that corner for any reason and peed right there on the carpet. I would watch shadows go by the curtains in the window and think it was the police, about to break in. I missed all my meetings and was cut off from the world, too scared to even move.

I dreaded turning on my phone and facing reality. When I finally did, I hadn't eaten for days and hadn't drunk a lot of water. My tongue was swollen, and I could barely breathe or talk. I got into my car, called Lisa,

---

B. Lisa: Sabe didn't have a turning point. It wasn't just one thing. But I do remember him saying that he did not want to pass the baton on to our kids. He wanted to change his life around. He wanted to get help. He didn't enjoy what he was doing. He wanted things to get better. He wanted to be a good dad. And I believed him. I really did.

C. Lisa: There were some good, happy times when we were living on the horse farm, days where he was present and enjoying the kids. We would take trips. We would go to New York City and the beach and things like that. That was all really good, but, I mean, it was always a little overshadowed with, "When is the next time going to happen?" The happiest times were just normal times when we were doing normal, everyday things. I learned how to hold onto really simple things.

and told her what had happened. She was clearly upset. She had been trying to get a hold of me for days and had called every hospital in the area.ᴰ My boss had been doing the same. I called my boss and told him that I had taken migraine medication that interacted badly with another medication I was taking and I had had to be hospitalized.

For the next few days, I struggled with severe depression and the consequences of my actions. I was eventually let go from that company because the market went down, but I was able to go back to the flooring company and help head up one of their largest accounts.

D. Lisa: Soon after Sabe left home, I tried getting hold of him, and I couldn't. That turned into a whole day of no contact. Then that turned into two days. I was so scared. His boss tried calling our home, and that made me even more scared because Sabe was supposed to be on a business trip. I actually looked online, found Sabe's credit card or bank statement, figured out what hotel he was staying in, called the hotel, and had them ring his room, but he didn't answer.

I think I tried dialing in his phone literally hundreds and hundreds of times. I really, really believed for a couple of days that he was dead. I was thinking ahead to, like, "I'm going to have to tell the kids how their dad died." I was thinking through to his funeral and his obituary. And then he called.

I felt total relief, like maybe we had been given another chance. I also thought, "Now I don't have to write his obituary or explain to our kids that their dad overdosed and that's how he died."

New Starts, Again

Lisa was tired of living in an old house and taking care of the 11-acre farm in Lovettsville.[E] She wanted a new start.[F] We found a house just down the road, in the heart of Lovettsville, and decided to own a home again.

I thought I was safe in my job, but as we were going through the process of buying the home and getting approved for a loan, I received a call from my boss and was laid off for the third time in two years. I had a call with the loan officer coming up that Friday and would have to verify my income, which meant I had to find a job very quickly—within three days.

Panic set in, and I spent the next two days responding to job ads. I came across an ad for a software sales job in the health care industry. It was based in Rockville, Maryland, about an hour's drive from Lovettsville. Within an hour or so of applying, I received a call to come in and interview the next day, the day before I had the appointment with the loan officer. I

E. Lisa: We had a lot of good memories there, but there were a lot of bad memories associated with it too at that point. And our kids were getting older. I wanted a driveway and a garage and a sidewalk and a closet—basic things. In the 1800s, when the house was built, if you had a closet, you were rich. So there was not much storage space. We had a shed where we would put a lot of stuff, but the mice got into everything. That was getting old, you know?

You have to understand, too, that we lived in that farmhouse for nine years and we were paying rent that entire time. It was that was kind of getting old to not be building up equity.

And it was too much maintenance. Sabe is not a fix-it man, nor is he a yard care kind of man. It was just time to move on.

F. Lisa: I don't think Sabe has relapsed again since we left the farmhouse. So it was definitely a fresh start.

drove down to Rockville, interviewed, and they offered me a position that same night. There was a huge problem though: They were offering half the salary I stated on the loan documents.

For a down payment, my mom gave us back all the cash that we had put into renovating the rental property and we borrowed money from Lisa's parents. Even with that, the loan officer chose not to approve the loan. Lisa was devastated.

Determined to be in a new home and a new environment, Lisa called her dad over the weekend and asked if he would co-sign on the loan with us. I felt terrible that we had to do that, and I didn't want to run the risk of not being able to pay for the mortgage. Half my salary would come from commissions, and I would be under a lot of pressure to close deals. Even though I was progressing with my disease, taking my medication, and not using anymore, the odds were stacked against us.[G]

But Lisa's dad agreed to help us, so we purchased the home and moved in. I was excited for my new career and started driving into Rockville that next week. I was still taking Seroquel and struggling to get up in the morning, but I consumed a lot of Diet Coke, and around 10-11 a.m., I would sneak out of work for twenty minutes for a quick nap in the car. Once my medication wore off, I had more motivation and was able to sell.

I was helping coach Shawn's football team in the fall, and between driving to Rockville and coaching, I drove about 170 miles a day. In the morning, I used that time to listen to scriptures. Listening to them would give me flashbacks from my past decade of trials. I felt terrible and had anxiety attacks. I had to learn to forgive myself and work through the memories and bad deeds, and even though I was always tired in the morning, I needed that long drive and spiritual nourishment so I could learn how to live with my actions.

Lisa was doing photography, and her business was flourishing. She even had a studio in downtown Leesburg. I was able to close a partner every week and earn enough with help from Lisa's business to pay all our bills. We even had enough to buy a new Toyota truck and an SUV for Lisa.

G. Lisa: I believe that my parents were always waiting for things to fail. They were always waiting to say, "We told you so." But now they really, really like Sabe. They really do. They very much appreciate that he has done so much to come out the other end.

In the fall of 2005, Chris and Alan Henricks invested in Horsey Farm, a 300-acre farm with a plantation-style home built in the late 1700s and renovated after the Civil War. The property was purchased for $2.8M with $1.4 being put down by Alan Henricks and Alan financing the balance. The deal was that Chris would make the $10,000 a month payment!

The home was in good condition, and Chris loved it. I continued to think that the deal would not solidify, and I did not concern myself with the venture. However, it did, and Chris and I planned to move. It was a big project because of the size of it and the type of furnishings it required. I agonized over it. However, as it turned out at the time, it was one of the peaks of the roller coaster and we located the furnishings for it. In retrospect from my perspective, it was a foolish move because all of the investment in it came from leveraging the Millcreek property. We took out $170,000 extra from the refinance, which was an interest-only loan, and we put the money into furnishing the house and making several of the $10,000 a month payments.

Of course, we could not keep up these payments for long, so they have been made by Alan. This is the property that Chris is currently trying to swing a big deal over in order to buy Alan out. I do not know all the details, and these are the sorts of things that I have tried to learn to detach from.

There are lots of crazy things going on at the farm at this time. There are three tenants who Chris has put into the houses. I do not think one of them has an actual lease. There are people who have their horses in the barns who are not paying rent. There are horses in the fields that are owned by people who do not take care of them, and Chris is left to feed and care for them. Chris has had a horse herd of up to 150 horses that he alone has cared for. Regardless of the fact that we live on a horse farm, no one can ride the horses because Chris is afraid of someone getting hurt!

Chris does not have a licensed vehicle to drive. His Ford truck has [expired] plates on it. The truck is ten years old and worn out, with 250,000 miles. He claims he has Farm tags for it, but he cannot take time to even put them on it.

In March of this year, I moved to the Millcreek farmhouse. I got tired of coming home to … a drunk husband. I could tell what kind of night I would have by the food on the floor by the refrigerator. The house would be dark and quiet, and oftentimes, the bedroom door would be locked. This was a sad and depressing situation, and I could not take it anymore, so on March 7, I moved my bed and clothing and stayed there up to the time that Chris went into treatment. At that time, I moved back into the house to be with Alec while he is caring for the farm while Chris is away.

Again, I was hoping while I was away that he would find his way back to AA. He did go to meetings on Saturday mornings when I went into Leesburg to go to Al-Anon. However, I am not aware of much activity beyond that, although he did claim he was going to start one at the farm! He would attend Al-Anon meetings with me in recent months on Tuesday and Wednesday nights. I always thought that strange, but thought perhaps anything was better than nothing.

I do think he has tried to quit without success. In September, his sons met with him twice to talk with him about getting help. He always assured them that he knew what he had to do. In the last two weeks, I finally gave up contact with him. I just could not take it anymore. It was the hardest thing in the world for me to not take a call or to hang up if the conversation was not going well.

Chris began to tell my sons that they did not really know who their mother was. He was accusing me of being dishonest with him, hinting that I was having an affair or something like that. The whole thing got so painful that I had to let go. I could see him spiraling out of control, and I began to look for treatment center options. Within a couple of weeks, we planned the intervention on Oct. 31, 2010.

During this time of progress for our little growing family, my father was struggling badly once again with alcohol. It always seemed that either my dad struggled or I did. We have had very few years where both of us were sober and doing well.

My mother and father were living in a 15,000 sq. ft. house in Burkettville on 300 acres. They had over 180 horses on three different farms, and my dad was one of the largest land brokers in the area. For years, we enjoyed the property they lived on. There were horses and 4-wheelers, and we would pick berries for fruit jams when they were in season. Thanksgivings, Christmases, and summers were amazing, but my dad's struggles were ever looming. He excelled at brokering land but couldn't stop the demons he faced. Eventually, the family decided to intervene once again.[H]

The day we confronted Dad was a wrestling match with the devil himself. We hired an interventionist to assist and tried remaining calm and to the script, but it quickly went south. Dad was very intoxicated, and he spewed evil comments. When the contention had reached its height, I grabbed him, pulled him into another room, and asked my brothers to follow. There, I told Dad I was going to give him a priesthood blessing.[1]

We all placed our hands on his head, and I pleaded with Heavenly Father to help. I felt moved to demand that the spirits surrounding and within him be removed, and as soon as I said those words, Dad dropped to the floor and started crying. He seemed to be a little more open, but it took a lot more to get him to accept help.

Lisa and his other daughters-in-law jumped in and threatened that he would never see the grandkids again unless he got help. It took a while for the alcohol to leave his system, but he eventually accepted help. He was quickly ushered away to the airport and shipped off to a rehab facility in Laguna, California.

H. Lisa: I definitely had a soft spot for Sabe's mom, but toward the end, before she passed away, I also was very resentful and angry toward her because she stayed in her marriage for so long. A lot of that frustration could have come from the tension that it brought to our own family. We would all be in the car and Chris would call Sabe or Sabe would call Chris, and then it would turn into screaming. I got to the point where I thought, "This is not good for our kids, to see you yelling at their grandpa."

1. In the Church of Jesus Christ of Latter-day Saints, a "priesthood blessing" is a way to call upon God to bless someone with healing, guidance, or comfort. To perform one, men who have authority to do so layer their hands on the recipient's head and one acts as voice to say the blessing. It is believed that the Holy Spirit often guides the words used.

> I am concerned about the next steps for Chris. I cannot imagine him coming back to this farm and all the problems. I cannot imagine us picking up our relationship at this point. I am definitely living one day at a time and am barely able to do that.[1]

When Dad returned home, he was okay for a few months, but as always, he started drinking again. Mom eventually moved out and began living by herself in an apartment in Reston.

Lisa started to think about selling our home and moving to Utah. I was growing stronger, and by that time, I was being recruited by other companies. I took a day off work to interview with one, and after a week, I was offered a job where I could work remotely. I accepted the job, we listed our house, and we started looking for a home in Utah.

After a few weeks, we bought one in Cottonwood Heights and moved in. Our new home was 5,900 feet above sea level and overlooked the entire Salt Lake Valley. This was the start of our family truly healing and thriving.[J]

I felt bad leaving Mom alone in Reston while my dad's drinking continued to spiral out of control, but I was glad to be away from it. We heard rumors that he had started visiting a female neighbor—he and Mom were still married—and knew he had gotten into a few fights over the property's management.

One of my mottos is to always have a pipeline at work and in your personal life—that is, always be building for your future. After losing my job so many times, I like to be prepared. I find myself squeezing every minute out of the day before I have to take my medicine at midnight to sleep. That is saying a lot for a bipolar person who, for so many years, didn't want to be alive.

---

1. Sabe: These were the last sentences in Mom's autobiography, ending with "barely able to do that." She gave her all to the very end of her life. She died eight years later, just four weeks after her divorce from Dad was finalized. The years from 2010 to 2018 saw her greatest struggle of all, and she wasn't able to write about it. It greatly saddens me.

J. Lisa: Sabe and I still work very well together as a team. I think we both work way too much, but I think we also want the good things in life, so we're willing to work hard for them. We have a lot to be grateful for.

I had the ability to work from home but decided it was best if I went to an office. I commuted to Provo and worked at three different companies full time simultaneously while building businesses on the side. I wanted so bad to be "normal" and to provide a good life for my kids and wife. I didn't want to be emotionally sick anymore. I was embarrassed by all the opportunities I had lost and all the friendships and lives I had negatively influenced.

At the same time, I was putting on a lot of weight because of my medication. I still had anxiety at night and would snack my way through it. Eventually, I stopped drinking caffeine, and four years later, I stopped consuming sugar, all in an effort to lose weight. Nothing I did seemed to help. I consistently put on weight, and I felt insecure about it. I wouldn't take off my shirt when we went to a public pool or beach, and I only wore black Nike golf shirts and stretchy pants from Costco. That "uniform," as my family, friends, and colleagues called it, was the only outfit I felt comfortable in until I had weight loss surgery in 2021 and lost ninety pounds. That is what it finally took to feel good in my skin again.

Ethan moved to Indianapolis and later to Utah, Dalton moved to Reno in 2014, and we convinced Mom to consider moving back to Utah and returning to our ancestral roots. Her job situation was deteriorating, and she wanted to be close to her grandchildren and her family. She found work writing grants and moved in with her mother, who was starting to need assistance. It was a perfect fit. She was only three hours' drive away from us and seven hours from Dalton.

Dad continued to live in the large Burkettsville manor, unable to maintain his health, the farm, and the house. We heard he would stay in one room and drink all day.

Emily

Dad's sisters made the trip across the nation to go rescue Dad from his terrible situation before Ethan and Dalton moved. When they arrived, they convinced him to pack his stuff and come back to live in Richfield, Utah, with his mom. He wouldn't have lived much longer if it wasn't for them driving out and forcing him to leave.

Dad fought to get back on his feet. He moved in with Mom and Grandma, which his sisters weren't very happy with. He would do well for short periods of time, but he always eventually relapsed. Once, he was binge drinking and I drove down to confront him. When I arrived at the house, he was playing the piano and being belligerent and verbally abusive. I told him he had to leave the house or I would call the police. I will never forget the looks he gave me and the words he muttered while playing the piano as if nothing was wrong. He seemed to be possessed and bound. I eventually called the police and had him removed from the home.

Over the next few weeks, he was homeless and living in a run-down hotel. Dalton felt impressed to do an intervention, so we found a place in Orem, Utah, that was covered by insurance and he agreed to go. When we picked him up from the nasty hotel, he had one dollar in his pocket. We dropped him off at a hospital to detox.

Mom was excelling in her job and securing grants for her employer at a record pace each year. She moved Grandma to a nursing home, and she would visit her every day, taking her to get her hair done on Thursdays.

Then, on September 10, 2016, I came home from a college football game and received a Facebook message from someone named Emily. It read, "Hey, hi Sabe, do you know who I am?"

I feel it is important that I let Emily tell her own story. This is what she's said about it:

> I was born in Wayne County and raised with the name Emily Hall. I grew up with four brothers, a mother, and a father. Everything was normal—until the fifth grade, when I was going through my baby book and I saw my birth certificate. It said, "Emily Roden." Who? I thought.
>
> It said my father was William Roden, and in my mind, I was like, I know that guy! He had daughters I went to school with. Once I made that connection, I didn't ask my mom about any of it. I just went to school, and at recess, I was all excited to tell the Roden girls, "Hey, did you guys know we're sisters?"
>
> They were like, "What?"
>
> "My birth certificate said your dad and my dad are the same! We're sisters!"
>
> By the time I got home from school that day, my mom had gotten a phone call from their mother saying, "What is going on?" So my mom sat me down and told me, "I was married to Bill at the time, so he's your dad." She said the dad I had when I was little—they had since divorced—had adopted me legally. She had hooked up with the dad I grew up with when she was nineteen and he was a senior in high school. His parents would not sign for him to get married to her, so she had my older brother outside of marriage. Then she started to date Bill Roden after my older brother was born, and they got married. Bill was my dad, but they didn't want to acknowledge it because it would cause trouble. She told me not to talk to his daughters about it anymore.
>
> I went to school with those girls for years. I was on the drill team and I played basketball and volleyball, and when Bill Roden would come to watch his kids, I'd think, "I wonder if he's proud of me?" I'd always smile at him, and when I'd see him at the store, I'd be really nice, but I was kind of timid around him. In the back of my mind, I was thinking, "Why does he not talk to me? Does he not love me?"
>
> For years, that's how it went.

At the same time, people in small towns talk and I kept hearing that my dad's name was Chris Anderson. I'd mention it to my mom once in a while, and she'd say, "People talk a lot. Those are just rumors." I learned to just deal with it.

In high school, I dated a boy, Jaron, who was the son of my mom's friend Gail. We kissed at my junior prom, and I mean, thank goodness that's all we did, was just kiss. Jaron had a good-looking cousin who would come around in the summer. His name was Dalton, and we made out twice, once in high school and again when I went to college and he was at BYU too. He was a good kisser.

I called my mom all excited afterward. She knew I was going with Jaron and Dalton, and so did Gail, and neither of them said anything—even though both of them knew that Chris was my dad and Dalton was my brother!

After I got married (to someone I'm not related to), my husband and I went to a wedding in Wayne County. A man walked into the church, and my husband said, "That's your dad."

I was like, "Whatever. You're so funny."

And he said, "If there's any guy in this whole world who's your dad, that's him right there. I can tell just by looking at him. Bill Roden's not your dad. You don't look anything like him."

I was twenty-four, and I finally started thinking, "That's true. I really don't look like him."

I looked at this other man and instantly had the weirdest feeling, because we did look alike!

My husband asked his grandma, "Who is that guy?"

She said, "Chris Anderson." It was like, "Oh my gosh! That's the name I keep hearing!"

By the time that wedding was over, I was beside myself. I couldn't think of anything but, "I gotta find out what is going on with this guy." I went straight to my mom and said, "I need to know the truth. I know this guy's my dad. Let's not beat around the bush anymore."

I was crying, and she started crying too and said, "It was hard to grow up and live here with all the rumors and gossip.

I didn't want to embarrass you or my family anymore." Then she told me the story of what had happened, that her car had broken down, Chris had stopped to help her while drunk, and then it had just happened. Chris had been married for six months and had a baby son—Dalton—on the way, and Mom was separated from Bill at the time, but they weren't divorced. She got pregnant, and since she didn't want to cause herself more embarrassment, she blamed it on Bill because they were legally still married. She said she told Chris, then he left town in the next few days and she didn't see him again.

Dalton was born in December of 1969, and I was born in July 1970. We're six months apart.

My husband and I lived near Chris's sister Angie, so I went to her house and talked to her about it. I said, "I really want to contact him and talk to him. What do you think?"

She said she had talked to Gail, their sister, and Gail's husband said we should just let this work out in Heaven and leave it alone for now. Gail said Chris was doing really good in life and he hadn't been drinking.

I was like, "I have no idea about any of that. I just want him to know that I know."

And she said, "We need to be hush about that and it will all work out in the end."

That was kind of like a smack in the face. Like, really? I don't matter enough to talk about in this world? It was hard, but I tucked it under and tried to forget about it.

A few years went by, and it never went out of my mind. I was always curious and didn't feel like I fit. Like, where do I belong? What are my roots? Why didn't he want me? Why wasn't I important to him?

My husband was the sheriff, and he called me one day and said, "You'll never believe who I just pulled over. Chris Anderson's wife."

Instantly, I was like, "Oh my gosh! What? Was Chris with her?"

He said, "Chris is still in Virginia. This would be a great time for you to try to reach out to him, because she's not gonna know."

I already had the Andersons' phone number from someone else, but I hadn't wanted to cause problems in their marriage. I got on the phone, and it rang a couple times before Chris answered.

I was thinking, "This is gonna be easy." Then I was like, "What am I gonna say?" So I just started saying, "This is Emily Ferguson. I don't know if you know me..." Stupid stuff. I don't even know what I said. He was kind of quiet, and then I said, "That is what my mom told me about what happened, and I just wanna see if you remember it the same way and if you could possibly be my dad."

He said, "Well, everything you just said is what happened, but I'm not sure if I'm your dad or not."

I said, "I want nothing from you, so don't think I'm calling to try to get anything. I just want to clear this from my mind and let you know I know." We talked for a few more minutes, and then we hung up and he said he would get back to me. I thought, "That was weird."

It really didn't solve anything, it didn't make me feel better, and of course, we never talked again.

I added Sabe and Dalton on Facebook, just out of curiosity. I wanted to snoop the family out. There were a few pictures with Chris on there, not a lot, but looking at their pictures was kind of fun. I'd think, "I look like Dalton. I look like Sabe."

My son Jayden has a drinking problem, has used all kinds of drugs, and has done anything bad you can think of. He's always said, "I just want to feel good in my head. I use stuff so that I can feel okay." He's been diagnosed with bipolar disorder, and every time we've thought he's at rock bottom, it's not rock bottom. Sabe would post sayings and stuff he'd write that I could relate to because of Jayden, and I'd lie in bed at night and cry while reading it. I thought, "I need to talk to this guy," but I was scared of rejection. I wondered if he and his family were going to be pissed or if they would hate me.

We were Facebook friends for years, and during that time, my husband and I moved into a camp trailer and began remodeling the house in front of my mom's. One night soon after Jayden had actually been put in jail, I read something

> Sabe had posted and I just couldn't get it off my mind. I thought, "I am saying it to him right now."
> So I did. It was the middle of the night, and I sent a message that said, "Do you know who I am?"
> It took Sabe a few minutes to respond, and I was thinking, "He's probably so mad right now."
> After a few minutes, I woke my husband up and said, "I just sent this to Sabe, and he hasn't said anything back."
> He was like, "It's been five minutes. It's okay."
> ... "Yeah, but why's it taking so long?"

Emily had my mother's maiden name and I knew she had lived in the town my parents grew up in, so I replied, "I'm sure we are cousins somehow, right?"

She replied, "LOL, well, not exactly, and it took me a while to figure things out and a long time to get to this point, to not care if I talk about it. But after I read your posts—not sure what trials you have been through, but it makes me sad and curious and has many emotions, so I feel like I want to reach out to you! I am your sister."

> It was, like, ten minutes again before he said anything, and I was just tense, lying in that stupid camp trailer going, "Is he going to answer back? What's he going to say? Oh I've really done it this time."

As you can imagine, I jumped out of bed. We have a sister?!^K

> Finally, Sabe and I just started talking. I could tell he was mad. It was like, "Are you kidding me?! What happened?!" We talked for hours.

K. Lisa: Sabe and I had just gotten in bed, and we were both on our phones. Then Sabe jumped out of bed and was like, "Lisa! Lisa! Lisa! Lisa!" There were so many emotions in his voice—there was shock and there was definitely some excitement, but I think he was mostly like, "Oh my gosh, I have a sister!" Oh, and he loves drama and there was some good juice happening.

He immediately called Dalton and said, "We have a sister!"
Dalton was like, "Please, please tell me it's not Emily."

The next day, I called the entire family and let them know. Then I drove to confront Dad about it in person. He had gone through thirty to sixty days of rehab at that time and was attending AA on a daily basis while living by himself in Dalton's townhome in Eagle Mountain, Utah. He downplayed the situation, but I told him he would need to do a DNA test and confront this head-on. He finally agreed to do that, so I met with Emily and collected a DNA swab, did the same with Dad, and sent the samples in. A few days later, the results came back positive. Dad was Emily's biological father.

> *It happened fast. The DNA test came back within a few days and proved that Chris was my dad. A couple days after that, they had a big party and we met the whole family and all their kids. It was wonderful. Everyone was so nice.*

When I asked Mom if she had known about Emily, she said people had told her about it a few times right after the incident (and again, years later). Hearing that was even a possibility had made her bend over with a terrible pain in her abdomen, and she had a mental breakdown. Then, when she inquired about it, she was lied to and snuffed by Dad and community members. She must have buried the thoughts deep inside in an effort to survive.

In her autobiography, written before the truth came out, she wrote:

> I had suspicions of Chris's drinking [while I was pregnant with Dalton]. On one occasion, I remember a rumor that shook me to the core. It involved him and another married woman. The story of a liaison between the two would surface from time to time, with her informing him that her husband was accusing him of being the father of her daughter Emily. Chris denied this at the time and continues to deny it to this day. Of course, I wanted to believe Chris and did at first, putting it out of my mind. But every once in a while, I question my naiveté. Sometimes, I wonder if drinking was involved and he does not remember what happened.
>
> I have questions of trust regarding this. Chris has been

> known to lie for lesser things, and I wonder if something like this is at the bottom of his subconscious and he tries to drown it with alcohol.

Mom had a hard time with all the lies that had kept her in the dark, but I will never forget her desire to include Emily and her family in all our family's gatherings.

I was scared to meet everyone, and I was thinking, "Chris has just come out of rehab. He's gonna start drinking again because of me." Then I felt guilt. Like, this is such bad timing. But Julia was really nice to me and to my kids, too. I don't think I would've been that nice. She met me in Richfield one day, I don't even know why, and we had lunch. She just wanted to have a talk with me and tell me how much she cared.

Goodbyes

Dad did begin drinking again, but his relapse probably had very little to do with Emily. Everyone always wanted Dad to have an excuse for why he continued to ruin his life, and while there were always little excuses, that's all they ever were—excuses.

He would frequently be drunk and belligerent at night when Mom came home, often bringing her to tears. At the same time, Dad was also trying to help raise money to fund a behavioral health group that provided classes and coaching, and it was very odd that he was drinking while engaged in trying to help people dealing with just that type of issue.

Alec divorced his wife and moved back in with our parents, which was a blessing to Mom for two reasons: first, he gave her comfort and companionship, and second, the move helped Alec get sober. He helped take care of Grandma, as well.

When Mom would come to visit me, we would have long talks about Dad. It is my belief that he wouldn't have accomplished what he did if it hadn't been for Mom. She truly lived day by day and in the moment, always trying to progress, always fighting. But by that time, there in my living room, she would break down and admit she couldn't handle him anymore. It broke my heart. I felt guilty for not supporting her more. I even felt guilty for wanting her to stay married to him. But I did feel grateful for my wife and how she has endured the hardships I have placed on her over all these years. Our entire family was coming to the conclusion that Dad would probably never stop drinking in this lifetime, and talking with Mom was when it finally sank in for me.

Just before my son Shawn left on a mission for the church, Mom decided to serve divorce papers to Dad and make him move out of the house. There was a three-month period for arbitration and to finalize the divorce, and it was a heartbreaking time for Mom, who still very much loved Dad but knew this had to be done.

We all worried about where he would go and what he would do. He was receiving only $700-$800 a month from Social Security, very little to survive on, and was facing lawsuit threats based on the accusation that he had misused capital he'd raised for a rehab and behavioral health facility in St. George. Would he end up homeless and sleeping in strange homes with people who didn't have his best interests at heart?

I thought it would be good to go visit my mom for the weekend, so I took Addie and asked Josh and his family if they would go with us, as well. One day during that visit, Josh, his family, Addie, and Mom went on a long hike in Snow Canyon. I stayed behind because of my weight and the heat, but I will never forget the fatigue I saw on my mom's face when she returned. She had obviously had fun, but she was dehydrated and her red face made it apparent that her body was tired. In a way, it was a synopsis of her life with her children and grandchildren: She would always sacrifice to support and enjoy her family.

Addie and I were the first to leave for home, and as we walked out the door and said goodbye, we hurried to the car through a curtain of rain. Mom followed us outside and stood in the rain to wave goodbye as we pulled out of her driveway.

That was the last time Addie and I saw Mom alive. The following day, Alec called us to say he thought Mom was having a heart attack. They had been eating dinner when she suddenly got up and went to lie down on her bed. He went to check on her, and she was in full-blown heart failure. He quickly called 9-1-1, and an ambulance arrived soon after.

As they drove to the hospital, Mom passed away.

My brothers and I decided to drive to the hospital. Dalton drove up from Vegas (where he was on a trip), and Josh, Ethan, and I piled into one car from Salt Lake. All I could think about was seeing her the day before, waving in the rain. In her hospital room, we offered a prayer and said our goodbyes.

In her home that night, we were all hungry. In what seemed like a miracle, there was enough food left over from the dinner she had cooked that night to feed all of us. She must have cooked enough for her and Alec to eat leftovers during the week. It was chicken cordon bleu, the same meal that she had cooked for my birthdays growing up in Virginia. It was a sweet, tender mercy and very humbling to realize that she had been able to feed her boys one more time.

We spent a lot of time preparing for the funeral that week, and having to deal with Dad made tensions run high. He did not come to the hospital and say his last goodbyes, and his drinking was at its worst. After a lot of disagreement between the siblings, we decided to let Dad back into the house as we prepared for the funeral. We focused on helping him get sober so he could attend the funeral in a respectful way.

The hardest part of the week was telling Grandma of her daughter's passing. Mom was the fourth child who had passed away before she did, and as we told her what had happened, she broke down.

The day of the funeral, all the boys talked and shared testimonies and memories of how amazing Mom was. There were countless stories of overcoming the odds, perseverance, grace, and sacrifice. She was laid to rest next to her older sister Alaina and some of their pioneer ancestors in a beautiful and small Utah town. When I was a teenager, we would visit Alaina's family in that area and work on their ranch in the summers. With red rock mountains surrounding it, Mom's grave was in the perfect setting.

Below are portions of the talk I gave at Mom's service.

> Mom was always teaching and being an example of progress, and although many of my memories were teaching moments from the trials that surrounded us, I want to share just a few memories that make me smile as well.
>
> Mom was an amazing cook. We never had many treats in the house, and if you didn't know how to combine food ingredients, you went hungry. She baked and cooked the proper way. I assume she was always so busy balancing kids, homework and the stress of her job, but we always teased her for burning one item while preparing for dinner each night. This happened so often that she actually acquired a love for burnt items like toast or whatever it may be. I believe she ate those to save the best for her hungry children.
>
> ... My mother and I had very deep and trying discussions. They were so emotional at times that for some reason, we could find irony, coincidence and humor in our

struggles. It was common to break out in gut-wrenching laughs during weight-bearing events. We seemed to use humor to cope. I loved that about her. We found joy in pain.

... My mother was led by the spirit of Moses and Lehi to take her family into the unknown. I love having this memory burned into my soul. In late December of 1981, Mom rented a U-Haul and finalized preparations for a move across the country to seek a different life for her boys and family. ... There was no job or pot of gold at the end, only hope. ... She had $2,000 in her bank and her father, John, as a driver.

... Virginia served its purpose in many ways, but the move is etched in my mind as a beacon of light during my trying times in life. I have had to endure mental illness, addiction, sin, and the many life struggles that we all face, and I will continue the fight of breaking cycles and bearing life as Mom did. I will follow the same light in the unknown wilderness that she did."

My mother emulated the light of Christ. She was blessed with the ability to see and do what was needed as she raised us. She radiated love, care, and understanding with unwavering faith. In troubled waters, she found safety for those around her. When in my darkest moments of disease, addiction, and sin, she stood as a beacon of truth, always ready to bring me back to the fold. She held the light high enough on the hill for me to see my way back home.

The week after the funeral, we had to return to our everyday lives. The stress of Mom's passing made me have a harder time sleeping; it seemed as if something inside me had cracked. The next time I visited the doctor, I asked him to increase my medication so I could sleep better. I had taken the same dosage for over a decade, and upping it that week showed me how fragile I really am.

My brothers and I had the burden of trying to secure shelter and a means for Dad to live. We had to sell Mom's home. We let him stay there in the meantime, but he brought a "bad spirit" to the home, he wouldn't keep the house clean, and he fought with us every time someone would come and look at the home. He even got in arguments with the real estate agents.

We eventually evicted him from Mom's home and found a condo in Parowan for him to stay in, paying cash for it so he wouldn't have a house payment. We redirected Mom's social security benefits into his name, and so with that, a clear budget, and no house or car payment, he was set up to ride out life.

If only it was that easy. Alec was staying with him in the condo, finishing his schooling at SUU, and he told us Dad's disease caused him to drink vodka around the clock and his friends were stealing TVs, money, and generally taking advantage of Dad. He was not fit to be on his own. Dalton sought to put adult protective care in place, but Dad refused. Then he met a woman who continued to come over and stay with him. Alec couldn't take anymore, and as soon as he finished school, he moved out.

However, Alec stayed in the area and continued to visit and help take care of Grandma. It was apparent she didn't have much time left on Earth, and eventually, just before COVID-19 hit the mainstream news, she caught what seemed to be pneumonia and passed away with her family around her.

As we approached the day of her funeral service, it was very apparent that Dad was struggling. He said he would come to the funeral, but we advised him that may not be a good idea because he would probably be drinking and make a scene.

While we drove in the procession following Grandma's hearse to her burial site, we got to Main Street and my eyes were drawn to a commotion at a gas station on the corner. Someone was being arrested. We continued on and said our goodbyes at the cemetery.

As we left Grandma's graveside service, I received a call. The person at the gas station had been Dad. He had driven two hours to get there while drunk, and when he arrived at that gas station, he had put his car in neutral then left it to enter the store. The car rolled back into the pumps, he caused a scene, and someone called the cops. The police were forced to get physical with him, and they arrested him. He received a DUI and spent over a week in jail before being released.

All my brothers were in the procession. We all passed the gas station. None of us noticed that the person being arrested was Dad. He was only a few yards away. It was a tender mercy, in my opinion, that we weren't distracted while honoring Grandma.

Dad and a woman he was seeing eventually moved into a small house in Parowan together and we sold his condo. He was becoming more and more distant from all the family. On one occasion, Ethan and I were returning from St. George with our kids and decided to stop by and see his house. Ethan and his family wouldn't go into the house and visit with him, so Shawn and I peeked in and spent ten minutes or so touring the home. Dad came out to the car to say "hi" to Ethan and his kids as we were leaving, but they ignored him.

Soon after that, Dad and his girlfriend were almost killed in a car accident and his girlfriend had to undergo physical rehabilitation to learn how to walk again. Then, just a month later, Dad was arrested on two counts of second degree felony and one count of first degree for assaulting a neighborhood girl. Earlier in the year, he had also been charged with a second degree felony for his business dealings and mishandling of funds. To say we were devastated and embarrassed is an understatement.

Dad spent two years in the county jail system. Since he would not plead his case or admit to any wrongdoing, he put the young girl, her family, and all of us through the process of a court trial by jury. He was found guilty on all counts, and in May of 2022, he was convicted and sentenced to seventeen years to life in prison. Nowhere in his trial or even as I talk to him now is alcohol mentioned. It's the proverbial "white elephant" in the room that has always lingered.

At this time, I am the only son who talks to him. The other members of our family have no desire to speak with him, and many have said that they feel like both our parents have passed on.

It's my prayer that all who suffer with addiction and mental illness will find the strength and courage to avoid the pitfalls of alcohol, drugs, and bad choices that keep us from reaching our potential. It has become very clear to me that taking control of my bipolar disorder and abstaining from substances has propelled my life forward in wonderful ways. I am no longer disconnected from responsibility and the mountain we must climb to blossom in life. I've gained momentum through little wins, and my support group has started to believe in me again and found ways to forgive me.

Many people inquire about the turning point in my life, wondering when and how I made the changes I have. To answer this, I use the analogy of unboiling a frog, which refers to the gradual process of being cooked (getting into trouble) over time without realizing it. In my case, this analogy worked in the reverse, where the change for the better was not brought about by a singular event, but rather a combination of various factors that worked together over time. As I progress and recover from bipolar disorder and my impulsive nature, I find myself frequently revisiting these steps, knowing that I'll need to continue doing so for the rest of my life. Without this foundation, I'm susceptible to mental illness and poor decision-making impulses.

I will expound upon these "Unboiling the Frog" steps in my upcoming book, a guide for coping with dual diagnoses (in my case, addiction and bipolar I).

As people with bipolar or addictions, we must take control of our journey. However, in my experience, the family members of those who suffer from mental illness and addiction seek help and understanding more often than those who are sick. I hope reading this story has been a positive experience.

If you are reading this and either have my genes or struggle with bipolar or addiction, my "two cents" in living a productive life are this: Turn your weaknesses into superpowers!

Grandpa & Friend, Sabe

HAPPY BIRTHDAY, MOM!
Love, Sabe & Family
(This book was finished on your special day)

Julia Anderson was raised in Utah, surrounded by farming culture, cattle ranchers, and the rich red rocks of Southern Utah. She earned a bachelor's degree in education from Utah State University and a master's degree from the University of Virginia. In the early '80s, she blazed across the United States and settled in Virginia, where she raised a family under her principles and values, with all her boys earning Eagle Scout awards and serving church missions. Julia had a deep-rooted sense of the importance of learning that culminated in a distinguished career in higher education. She was a passionate member of the Church of Jesus Christ of Latter-day Saints and lived faithfully until her passing.

www.ingramcontent.com/pod-product-compliance
Lightning Source LLC
Chambersburg PA
CBHW050329010526
44119CB00050B/732